TRANSITIONS

OTHER BOOKS BY WILLIAM BRIDGES

Managing Transitions

JobShift

Surviving Corporate Transition

The Character of Organizations

A Year in the Life

Creating You & Co.

The Way of Transition

SECOND EDITION

TRANSITIONS

Making Sense of Life's Changes

WILLIAM BRIDGES, PH.D.

Da Capo
LIFE
LONG

A Member of the Perseus Books Group

Text design by Brent Wilcox
Set in 11 point Electra by the Perseus Books Group

Cataloging-in-Publication data for this book is available from the Library of Congress.

First Da Capo Press edition 2004
ISBN-13 978-0-7382-0904-3
ISBN-10 0-7382-0904-X

Published by Da Capo Press
A Member of the Perseus Books Group
http://www.dacapopress.com

Da Capo Press books are available at special discounts for bulk purchases in the U.S. by corporations, institutions, and other organizations. For more information, please contact the Special Markets Department at the Perseus Books Group, 11 Cambridge Center, Cambridge, MA 02142, or call (800) 255-1514 or (617) 252-5298, or e-mail special.markets@perseusbooks.com.

19 20

To all the people in transition that I have worked with during the past 30 years.

CONTENTS

ACKNOWLEDGMENTS

This book represents a personal inquiry into a confusing aspect of my own experience. My original intent was to make sense out of unexpected changes in my own life, and only after that to begin working with others who felt the same need—and only then, belatedly to write a book. Hence my acknowledgments go not to people who helped me with a book or with a formal piece of research, but to people who helped me with my own transitions.

That represents a very large group of people, and I'm tempted to get out my address book and begin ticking off names. Instead, I want to list a very few people who played key roles in the book's creation. The late James Ingebretsen offered me support at a number of crucial points during the writing of the first edition, and so did John Levy, who acted as an unofficial editor on the project. My late wife, Mondi, helped me throughout the writing project and taught me a great deal from her experience as a psychotherapist. Then my Da Capo editor, Marnie Cochran, first imagined this new and revised edition, and saw it through to its publication. And finally, my wife, Susan, who read the original book before we ever met and is now the solid rock in my own sea of transitions.

PREFACE TO THE SECOND EDITION

In the twenty-five years since this book was first published, my own life has gone through many (sorry, but there's no better word for it) *transitions* that I could not have foreseen when I originally wrote the book. In 1979, I was still an ex-literature teacher, but after *Transitions* I started a new career as a person who helped others deal with the changes in their lives. This little book got me launched.

At the time the book originally came out, I hardly imagined what could happen. I worried, in fact, that *Transitions* was too insubstantial to attract many readers or to stay in print for long. But now, twenty-five years, forty-one printings, and more than half a million copies later, it's alive and well. Amazing! And just as amazing, with all those copies in print, I have never come across one in a used-book store, although I often cruise the shelves of such places. I know from countless conversations with readers that people keep the book and reread it whenever a significant change hits them. They also pass the book on to their friends—who sometimes don't return it, but keep it to be ready for *their* next change or to pass it on to *their* friends. So there's no telling how many people have read the book.

From the beginning, however, some things about the book dissatisfied me. There was a chapter called "Love and Work," and I thought that I hadn't said enough about the ways in which those two critical areas of life can put you in transition, not to mention how being in transition can affect your relationships or career. I also wished there were some way to add further thoughts to the book, thoughts that were based on all the work I had done after the book was published. And finally, in a few places I felt that I hadn't been quite clear and wanted another shot at explaining myself.

There was another problem with the first edition: I had published it when I was in my mid-forties. Today, as I turn seventy, things look a bit different to me. Not surprisingly, the natural transitions produced by aging are more on my mind now than they were back then. I'm also fascinated by the profound re-conception of "retirement" that is going on today. Yet even those creative reinventions of retirement usually view retirement as a *change* rather than as a *transition*.

But that is partly my own fault. I don't think I made the *change/transition* distinction clear enough in the first edition. Our society confuses them constantly, leading us to imagine that *transition* is just another word for *change*. But it isn't. *Change* is your move to a new city or your shift to a new job. It is the birth of your new baby or the death of your father. It is the switch from the old health plan at work to the new one, or the replacement of your manager by a new one, or it is the acquisition that your company just made.

In other words, *change* is situational. *Transition*, on the other hand, is psychological. It is not those events, but rather the inner reorientation and self-redefinition that you have to go through in order to incorporate any of those changes into your life. Without a transition, a change is just a rearrangement of the furniture. Unless transition happens, the change won't work, because it doesn't "take." Whatever word we use, our society talks a lot about change; but it seldom deals with transition. Unfortunately for us, it is the transition that blind-sides us and is often the source of our troubles.

It is, thus, no accident that people imagine that they can prepare for, say, retirement by making adequate financial preparations, choosing a good place to live, and developing some new "interests." In those articles about retirement, you don't find anything about going through that three-phase transition process that this book deals with—or how little getting all set for the *change* prepares you for the *transition*.

Some other societies have paid much more attention to transition than we have, and in doing so they prepared people much more effectively for the experience of being in transition than our society has prepared us. Those societies typically had rituals (we call them "rites of passage") to help individuals let go of their outlived life-chapter and find a new one to replace it. They also had transition-punctuated concepts of the lifetime which prepared people to expect transitions to come along to come along at certain times. Lacking such concepts, we are like people with no idea of the year's natural seasons. We notice that it gets colder and warmer, wetter and dryer, but we chalk that up to the daily ebb and flow of "weather." We miss the larger picture.

The seasonal analogy suggests another way that traditional societies taught people about transition. Most of those societies had fairly elaborate seasonal rituals to mark the point where the days stopped growing longer and started getting shorter, or the point where one year stopped and the next year started. Oh, we have New Year's Eve and New Year's Day, but those are little more than occasions for a party or a day in front of football games on TV. Our New Years' celebrations do not give us a real experience of the world *dying* and being *reborn*.

Other societies, in short, regularly and repeatedly dramatized the transition process, which was the way that *how-the-way-things-*

had-been ended in a kind of death, and a new *way-things-are-going-to-be* took its place through a sort of birth. Through those dramatizations, people grew familiar with transition and learned how to handle it. You can wish that we had such rituals and celebrations, but we do not. We are going to have to learn to do individually and consciously for ourselves what once was done for people automatically and collectively by their society.

At the time I first published this book, I entertained the fantasy that I might someday launch a whole new profession. I even had a name for it: *maieutics*. Derived from the Greek word for "midwife," maieutics (as I imagined it) was the name for the assistance that a professional could provide people who were struggling with the death-and-rebirth process of transition. As it turned out, there were hundreds of thousands of people out there who were trying to make sense out of transition, but far fewer that wanted to be in the business of facilitating death and rebirth. ("Death and rebirth? Isn't that a little . . . uhh . . . drastic? Don't you have just some techniques for changing careers—or going through a divorce, or turning forty, or . . . whatever? Maybe a How-To manual?")

So the new profession did not emerge; but I went through the transition I was then in—the one that had led to the writing of this book in the first place. And I did build a new career for myself as someone who helped individuals and organizations handle the personal side of change (called *transition*) so that it is less distressing and disruptive and more productive. My own transition back in the seventies was the point at which I re-created myself. Your own transition (the reason you decided to look into this book, remember?) can do the same for you.

I wish you well on your journey.

PART I

THE NEED FOR CHANGE

The nine cities of Troy, each built on the ruins of its predecessor, were accumulated over millennia, from the Stone Age till Roman times. Pompeii was buried by volcanic eruption. . . . The Old World thus had its ghost towns, but more often than not they were buried and men built on the rubble of their ancestors' disappointed hopes. In America the archaeology of fast-moving men on a nearly empty continent was spread plain and thin on the surface. Its peculiar product was the abandoned place (the "ghost town") rather than the buried place. Its characteristic relics were things left by choice before they were used up.

—DANIEL J. BOORSTIN
The Americans: The National Experience[1]

AMERICANS HAVE ALWAYS BEEN IN TRANSITION. Whereas Old World families trace themselves back to a place, New World families originate in an act of migration. Nor did the transition from an old life to a new one end when the immigrants arrived on these shores. From place to place and job to job, Americans kept moving. Drawn forward by the faith that better things lay just beyond the horizon, they lived a life marked by frequent transitions. European visitors often noted this and marveled that Americans seemed to thrive on it. In 1831, Alexis de Tocqueville, the great French student of American life, mentioned the trait in his diary:

> Born often under another sky, placed in the middle of an always moving scene, himself driven by the irresistible torrent which draws all about him, the American has no time to tie himself to anything, he grows accustomed only to change, and ends by regarding it as the natural state of man. He feels the need of it, more, he loves it; for the instability, instead of meaning disaster to him, seems to give birth only to miracles all about him.[2]

That, at least, was one half of the American story—the outer, the "official" half. Inwardly, this experience of being in transition was not so comfortable. Like old Rip van Winkle, countless Americans "woke up" to the impact of change on them at some point in their lives. Old Rip, you remember, had been put under a spell, so he had an excuse. But for those who had been seeking transitions as a pathway to self-advancement, the experience was puzzling. When he was fifty, Henry Wadsworth Longfellow, the most famous American writer of his day, went back for a visit to his hometown of Portland, Maine. While there, he wrote a poem called "Changed"; here are the opening stanzas:

> *From the outskirts of the town,*
> *Where of old the mile-stone stood,*
> *Now a stranger, looking down,*
> *I behold the shadowy crown*
> *Of the dark and haunted wood.*
>
> *It is changed, or am I changed?*
> *Ah! The oaks are fresh and green,*

But the friends with whom I ranged
Through their thickets are estranged
By the years that intervene.[3]

In the century and a half since that poem was written, the pace of change in American life has speeded up greatly. As Alvin Toffler wrote in *Future Shock*, "Change is avalanching upon our heads and most people are grotesquely unprepared to cope with it."[4] (That statement, being thirty-five years old, is presumably also out of date!)

But it is not just the pace of change that leaves us disorientated. Many Americans have lost faith that the transitions they are going through are really getting them somewhere. To feel as though everything is "up in the air," as one so often does during times of personal transition, is endurable if it *means something*—if it is part of a movement toward a desired end. But if it is not related to some larger and beneficial pattern, it simply becomes distressing.

Moreover, the experience of being in transition is itself changing. Being in between marriages or careers takes on a particularly painful quality when those things are changing profoundly. It is as if we launched out from a riverside dock to cross to a landing on the opposite shore—only to discover in midstream that the landing was no longer there. (And when we looked back at the other shore, we saw that the dock we had left from had broken loose and was heading downstream.) Stuck in transition between situations, relationships, and identities that are also in transition, many Americans are caught in a semipermanent condition of transitionality.

One might imagine that writers and counselors would have addressed themselves to this situation long ago. But that is not so. If you go to the library and look up *transition* in the subject index, you will probably find that the headings skip from *transit systems* to *translation*—nothing on *transition*. Of course, there are entries under *divorce, bereavement,* and *careers, changing;* and a good deal is available on important specific life changes, but nothing on the inner and underlying process of transition itself.

It is true that back during the decade before *Transition* first appeared, a crop of books on adulthood had been published that at least justified the difficulties we experienced as "Catch-30" or the "Mid-Life Crisis." But such books were based on idealized life schedules that hung off us like one-size-fits-all clothes, so they did little to clarify the actual experience of being in the midst of transition.

The subject of this book is the difficult process of letting go of an old situation, of suffering the confusing nowhere of in-betweenness, and of launching forth again in a new situation. Because those three phases are going to be so critical to what we are discussing, let me reiterate: All transitions are composed of (1) an ending, (2) a neutral zone, and (3) a new beginning. Drawing on modern research into adult development, I'll give you some useful ways of thinking about why transition occurs when it does. Recognizing that every lifetime has its own unique rhythm, *Transitions* provides the tools for identifying a personal developmental chronology. Cutting through the particulars of specific changes, the book identifies transition's characteristic impact on work and relationships. Finally, it provides concrete ways for people to help themselves deal constructively with times of transition.

Transitions is not simply a manual on how to cope; rather, it is based on a theory of personal development that views transition as the natural process of disorientation and reorientation marking the turning points in the path of growth. Throughout nature, growth involves periodic accelerations and transformations: Things go slowly for a time and nothing seems to happen—until suddenly the eggshell cracks, the branch blossoms, the tadpole's tail shrinks away, the leaf falls, the bird molts, the hibernation begins. With us it is the same. Although the signs are less clear than in the world of feather and leaf, the functions of transition times are the same. They are key times in the natural process of development and self-renewal. Without an understanding of such natural times of transition, we are left impossibly hoping that change will bypass us and let us go on with our lives as before. If we have learned one thing since *Transitions* was originally published, it is that change will happen—that change is the norm now, and somehow or other we will need to develop ways of dealing productively with it.

Being In Transition

"Who are you?" said the Caterpillar. . . .
"I—I hardly know, Sir, just at present," Alice replied rather
shyly, "at least I know who I was when I got up this morning,
but I think I must have changed several times since then."

—LEWIS CARROLL
Alice's Adventures in Wonderland[1]

I BECAME INTERESTED IN THE SUBJECT OF TRANSITION around 1970 when I was going through some difficult inner and outer changes. Although I gave up my teaching career because of those changes, I found myself teaching a seminar called "Being in Transition." (Rule number one: When you're in transition, you find yourself coming back in new ways to old activities.) The twenty-five adults who showed up for that course were in various states of confusion and crisis, and I was a bit at sea myself. I had, after all, left my career and moved my family to the country, where we joined several other families and formed a small community. I had set out to change my lifestyle.

I had imagined, I think, that the seminar would attract mostly other exurbanites and that together we could puzzle out this difficult transition. A few of these new country folk were in the class, but the mix was far richer than that. There were men and women who had recently divorced or separated. There were a couple of newlyweds as well as some people who had remarried, one a twenty-six-year-old man who had suddenly acquired four children. There was a widow and several recently retired men. There was the wife of a retired man (who didn't attend the seminar because his health had worsened a few weeks after his retirement).

There was a woman who had just given birth to her first baby; a man who had just had a heart attack; and even a man who had recently received a big promotion at work. ("What is *he* doing here?" the others asked resentfully. "*He* doesn't have problems.") There were three or four women who had just returned to college after years of raising children. There were two people who had just been fired. And there was a young woman who was living on her own for the first time. She was appalled to find that the rest of us, her elders, didn't have our lives in better shape. "It's OK to be messing around when you're twenty-three," she said, "but I plan to get it all together by the time I'm your age." (We all nodded sheepishly and admitted that we had planned it that way, too.)

At first, the seminar members were shy with each other and took refuge in the claim that they did not really have much in common. ("*You* still have your job." "Well, *you're* luckier. You still have your marriage.") But slowly they began to discover that, under the surface, their situations challenged them to deal with the same basic experience. As we listed them on the board the first night, the three main similarities seemed to be that we had all experienced (1) an ending, followed by (2) a period of confusion and distress, leading to (3) a new beginning, for those who had come that far.

Each person's attitude toward what we began talking about as the three phases of transition differed considerably, of course. Those who had chosen to make the changes that had put them into transition tended to minimize the importance of endings; it was almost as if the act of acknowledging an ending as painful was an admission that the change triggering the transition had been a mistake. On the other hand, those who had gone into transition unwillingly or unwittingly found it very hard to admit that a new beginning and a new phase of their lives might be at hand. They were as invested in seeing no good in their transition as the other group was in denying distress. But they all agreed that the in-between place was strange and confusing. They hoped to get out of it, in favor of either the Good Old Days or the Brave New World, as quickly as possible.

We decided to study these three phases of transition, and I announced that *endings* would be the topic of the seminar's second session. This dismayed the new mother. "I'm not sending him off to college," she said, "just trying to get used to having him." She was trying to cope with beginnings, not endings. He was, of course, a *wonderful* little baby (she repeated that several times), but she was having some small problems. How much should she let him cry, she asked her classmates, and how could she persuade her husband to help more?

In seconds, the air was thick with advice and we were drifting away from *endings* fast. Interestingly, though, our advice was of little use because she had heard it all before—had even read most of it before the baby arrived. This upset her and she grew angry, first with her husband, and then with her mother, who hadn't told her what mothering was really like, and then with the baby, and finally with us for "sitting there and nodding and acting sympathetic, when you don't give a damn if I'm falling apart—and I *am* falling apart!"

It was clear that we had come a long way from that *wonderful* little baby that she needed a tiny bit of advice about. But we also seemed to be getting somewhere, for in the next few minutes she talked very movingly about her life and her desire for children. She and her husband had been married for two years before she became pregnant, and they had been very happy together. Both of them had wanted children, but each of them was startled to find a fussy new infant so intrusive and demanding. "We aren't alone together any more," she said sadly, after her anger had passed. "I really do love the baby, but the old freedom and easiness are gone. We can't take off any longer whenever we please, or even live by our own schedules. I feel like it isn't even my own life I'm living."

This woman, who had wanted us to forget endings and get on to beginnings, was being confronted with the impact of several endings in her life. The problems that we hadn't been able to solve for her proved to be less important than she had first claimed, for no matter what happened to them, the underlying situation would remain. "I never thought of it this way," she said, "but now it seems to me that I've crossed some kind of threshold and there's no going back. My old life has gone. How come nobody talks about that? They congratulate you on your new life, but I have to mourn the old life alone."

In fact, this wasn't so. For as soon as she had put her predicament into words, half a dozen people echoed her experience and gave their versions of it. So why was it so difficult to talk about? For some people, it was the shame they felt for being sad or angry about a supposedly "good thing"; for others, it was remorse over lost opportunities. And for still others, it was simply the confusion and embarrassment over not being able to manage an ordinary life experience smoothly—something they imagined that others did easily. For all these reasons, they found it hard to talk about the unexpected impact of an ending in their lives—and the way in which that unacknowledged ending impeded their ability to move toward a new beginning.

And thus we came to rule number two: Every transition begins with an ending. We have to let go of the old thing before we can pick up the new one—not just outwardly, but inwardly, where we keep our connections to people and places that act as definitions of who we are. There we are, living in a new town, but our heads are full of all the old trivia: where the Chinese restaurant was (and when it opened in the evening), what Bob's phone number was, what shoe store stocked the children's sizes, and when the doctor took his day off. No wonder those tribal rites of passage in which the group facilitates a person's transition from one life phase to the next often contain rituals for clearing the mind of old memories and information.[2]

We usually fail to discover our need for an ending until we have made most of our necessary external changes. There we are, in the new house or on the new job or involved in a new relationship, waking up to find that we have not yet let go of our old ties. Or, worse yet, *not* waking up to that fact, even though we are still moving to the inner rhythm of life back in the old situation. We're like shellfish that continue to open and close their shells on the tide schedule of their home waters after they have been transplanted to a laboratory tank or the restaurant kitchen.

Why is letting go so difficult? This is a puzzling question, especially if we have been looking forward to a change. It is frightening to discover that some part of us is still holding on to what we used to be, for it makes us wonder whether the change was a bad idea. Can it be that the old thing was somehow (and in spite of everything we thought we knew) right for us and the new thing wrong?

These questions arise particularly when a person's life situation is not an especially happy one. The full-time mother who finally decides to break the narrow bounds of housecleaning and carpooling by taking a part-time job, or the bored office worker who gets a chance to join the staff of a newly formed company—these people hardly expect to find the old roles difficult to shed. And the person who has been estranged from parents or siblings for years won't expect to be profoundly shaken by their deaths. How can we feel a "loss" when we marry after years of loneliness or receive an inheritance after struggling to make ends meet or achieve fame after a career spent trying to make it?

The old radio comedian, Bob Burns ("The Arkansas Traveler"), used to tell the story of eating army food for the first time after eighteen years of his mother's deep-fat frying. A week of bland GI fare was enough to cure something he had never realized he suffered from: heartburn. But rather than feeling relief at his improvement, Burns rushed into the dispensary, clutching his stomach and yelling, "Doc, doc! Help me! I'm dying. My fire went out!"

We feel these unexpected losses because, to an extent that we seldom realize, we come to identify ourselves with the circumstances of our lives. Who we think we are is partly defined by our roles and relationships, those we like as well as those we don't. But the bonds go deeper even than that. Our whole way of being—the personal style that makes you recognizably "you" and me "me"—is developed within and adjusted to fit a given life pattern. The very complaining that we do is part of that style. To hear Marge talk about Jack's inattentiveness, or to hear Jack talk about never really being given a chance to show his stuff at work, you would think they would jump at the chance to change. But then Jack brings home flowers, and Marge says, "What's wrong? I know that something's wrong!" And Jack is given an important assignment of his own and finally has the chance to get the attention that he has sought for so long, and he finds several things wrong with the deal.

Jack may say to Marge (or the boss may say to Jack), "See, you really don't want to change. You like to gripe, but when you get the chance, you mess it up or chicken out." And that is half true—but only half. For the wanting is true, too, and the desire for change is also really true. Transitional situations bring this paradox to the surface and force us to look at negative and positive aspects of our life situations.

There are ways of facilitating transitions, and they begin with recognizing that letting go is at best an ambiguous experience. They involve seeing transition in a new light, of understanding the various phases of the transition. They involve developing new skills for negotiating the perilous passage across the "nowhere" that separates the old life situation from the new. But before that can be done, you need to understand your own characteristic ways of coping with endings.

One way to do this is to think back over the endings in your own life. Go back to your early childhood and recall the first experiences involving endings that you can remember. Some may have been large and terrible—deaths in the family, for instance; others may have been insignificant to everyone except you—your parents' departure on a trip, the death of a pet, or a friend's moving away. Continue forward on this tour of your life history and note all the endings you can recall along the way. Some were physical; others involved relationships inside and outside the family. Some involved places, social groups, hobbies, interests, or sports; others involved responsibilities, training, or jobs. Some endings may be hard to describe. They have few outward signs, but they may leave long-lasting scars: the ending of innocence or trust, for example, or the ending of irresponsibility or of a religious faith. How many such endings can you retrieve from your memory?

As I said, we all develop our own typical response to ending things. The inner element in that response is a mental state or mood or frame of mind. Like the air we breathe, that mood can be so familiar that it is difficult to identify. But it helps to think back on old endings and to try to recall the feelings and thoughts you had then. As you begin to remember your old reactions to endings, you are likely to realize that your old mindset is being reactivated in the present whenever something ends in your life. Leaving for a better job may, ironically enough, cause the same grief and confusion that occurred in the past when you reached the sad end of a core relationship. It is important to recognize this, for it means that some of the feelings you experience today have nothing to do with the present ending but are the product, instead, of the resonance set up between situations in your present and those in your past.

What you bring with you to a transitional situation is the style you have developed for dealing with endings. The product of early experience and late influence, this style is your own way of dealing with external circumstances and with the inner distress they stir up. Your style is likely to reflect your childhood family situation, for transitions tend to send family members off to different tasks: One person feels all the grief and anxiety for the entire group, another comforts the mourner, another takes over the routine responsibilities, and yet another goes into a sort of parody of "being in control of the situation."

Somewhere along the way, you may also have picked up somebody else's style and copied or adapted it to your situation. Do you remember, for instance, Woody Allen's Humphrey Bogart "ending" in *Play It Again, Sam*, which consisted of saying "Sssso long, ssssweetheart," and then lighting a cigarette and walking off alone into the night?

Looking back over your ending experiences, what can you say about your own style of bringing situations to a close? Is it abrupt and designed to deny the impact of the change, or is it so slow and gradual that it is hard to see that anything important is happening? Do you tend to be active or passive in these terminal situations? That is, is it your initiative that brings things to term or do events just happen to you? Some people learn early to cultivate a subtle sort of receptivity to coincidence, or they become skilled at covertly inviting other people to act upon them when change is in the wind.

These people are characterized by a kind of blamelessness in regard to endings. They had no choice, they seem to say. The situation was beyond their control. In that first class on transition, we had several Blameless Ones, and they irritated everyone. None of us was feeling quite like the master of our fate, but most of us acknowledged having played some part in the transition we were experiencing. Not the Blameless Ones, though, and particularly not the man whose wife had recently left him. ("She just walked out— no warning, no nothing—just left me.") He resented the idea that his own style might be one of inviting endings. He figuratively showed us his hands. ("See—clean.") And like someone who shouts "I didn't do it" when the police arrive, he called attention to himself and made everyone suspicious. He never caught on to what the others meant, and he finally stopped coming to class—another ending that he couldn't help—when one of the women *insulted* him by calling him "emotionally accident-prone." Rule number three: Although it is advantageous to understand your own style of endings, some part of you will resist that understanding as though your life depended on it.

If this process of recollection activates that part of you, you'll find it hard to remember past endings or to see that you have a characteristic way of responding to them. Let that be. Just note your difficulty and try a different approach to the same question. Think about how you tend to act at the end of an evening at a friend's house or a night on the town. Do you try to drag things out by starting new conversations and activities as others seem to be ready to leave, or do you say suddenly that it was a nice evening and dash out? Or what about some recent larger ending: leaving a job or moving from a neighborhood. Did you say goodbye to everyone, or did you leave a day ahead of schedule just so that you could avoid the goodbyes?

Everyone finds endings difficult, so your own style is not a sign that you have some "problem" that others don't have. The person who leaves early and the one who stays late are both avoiding endings and the discomfort of facing a break in the continuity of things. Whether you are a dasher or a lingerer is largely the result of how you learned to avoid the "party's-over" experience as a child. You might, on the other hand, have learned back then that although some endings are unavoidable they do not usually bring unendurable distress, and that dealing with them at the time avoids difficulty later; you are likely to try to take the experience one step at a time, saying your goodbyes and moving on to whatever comes next.

However you learned to deal with them, endings are the first phase of transition. The second phase is a time of lostness and emptiness before "life" resumes an intelligible pattern and direction. The third phase is that of beginning anew.

We shall discuss the in-between time in detail in Chapter 6, so we'll move along here to the question of beginnings. You also have your own characteristic way of beginning things, and you can learn something about it by thinking back over your past, starting with early childhood, just as you did with endings. Imagine that you were writing an account of your life. At what points could you use the phrase "A new chapter in my life opened when . . ."?

For some people, these times of change and renewal always seem to involve new relationships, but for others they involve new places or projects. For still others, it is some new state of mind that appears first, a new feeling or self-image or goal. Sometimes the beginning results from careful and conscious effort, but for most people important new beginnings have a mysterious and sometimes accidental quality to them. That is interesting because most of us think we ought to "take charge" of our lives and "plan carefully" when we're trying to start again after an ending. As we shall see later, most of us do that prematurely, for our most important beginnings take place in the darkness outside our awareness. It is, after all, the ending that makes the beginning possible.

So we have rule number four: First there is an ending, *then* a beginning, and an important empty or fallow time in between. That is the order of things in nature. Leaf-fall, winter, and then the green emerges again from the dry brown wood. Human affairs flow along similar channels, or they would if we were better able to stay in that current. But endings make us fearful. They break our connection with the setting in which we have come to know ourselves, and they awaken old memories of hurt and shame. Growing frightened, we are likely to try to abort the three-phase process of ending, lostness, and beginning. We might even twist this pattern around so that beginnings come first, then endings, and then . . . then what? Nothing. When we turn things around in that way, transition becomes unintelligible and frightening.

One of the benefits to reviewing your experience of endings is to see how often they have cleared the ground for unexpected beginnings. But reviewing these elements in your past may also uncover the times when the ending did not provide a starting point, as well as times when you started a new journey without unpacking your baggage from the old one. Right now, at this new transition point in your life, remember some of these aborted transition points from your past. Poke around among them as you might explore an old house you once lived in. Some of these unfinished transitions might be ones that you could still complete, and if you did that, you would bring more energy and less anxiety to your present situation as a result. Completion may involve no more than a belated farewell, a letter, or a call to someone. It may involve an inner relinquishment of someone who outwardly you left behind years ago, or some old image of yourself, or some outlived dream or outworn belief that you have kept in your baggage long past its time. You'll travel more easily if you lighten your load.

Most of us can do a great deal to finish up with the past, but when we have done that we are back in the present, with all its ambiguities. In the midst of the change, it is not easy to say just what is ending and what else may emerge to take its place. One day everything seems to be coming apart; the next day, life goes on as usual, and we wonder whether we have been imagining our difficulties. We try to get our bearings by looking for markers: How far have things actually changed, and what is the real result of the change on our lives?

One of the reasons it is so difficult to assess these things is that the impact of transition upon us does not necessarily bear any relation to the apparent importance of the change that triggered it. One person may be brought to a complete standstill by a divorce or a job loss, but another person may take it in stride. Someone else may come to terms with a debilitating illness and then be demolished by the loss of a beloved pet.

In that first transition class, I learned more about what accounts for these differences from the class member whose only apparent life change was his promotion at work. He was in great distress, although he did not know why, and the rest of the class tended to make light of it. The promotion itself was working out all right, he claimed, but there was still some nameless change that threatened to wreck his life. We ran through the obvious categories: His finances were stable, his health was generally good, his kids were doing well in school, his career was fine. "Nothing's wrong," he said irritably, and the rest of the class eyed him suspiciously, as though he might be a spy.

But then, as we moved past the idea of "a promotion" to the reality of his life situation, a different picture began to emerge. The promotion was just the tip of the iceberg, for the man's company had undergone a major reorganization. The man's position had been shifted to a newly created division in the company, and his old boss, who had also been a good friend, had been fired. The man's new role required him to report to a new set of superiors, and he was not yet sure what they thought of him. "I keep wondering if they'll hang on to me long enough to get through the changes and then fire me too," he said.

The new job had two immediate effects on his home life. First, it required that he work longer hours; and second, it gave him a big pay raise. The new income, together with a mortgage that he really wished he hadn't taken out, had led to a major remodeling job at home. "I don't like the way we're suddenly spending so much more, and I try to explain that to my wife, but she just says that we've waited and waited for this, and now we ought to enjoy it." Life at home was, in fact, punctuated by many more arguments than in the past. He disapproved of her spending, and she disapproved of his new work schedule.

The longer hours had repercussions elsewhere as well. His children complained that the family never did anything together anymore, and his in-laws complained that he was always too busy to bring the family down for visits. Everyone objected to the way he now wanted to spend his spare time, for his new business associates encouraged his old interest in golf and this effectively brought an end to family camping trips.

"Then, just after I got the promotion, I got sick," the man said with a weary shake of the head. "Some timing! It was some strange virus, and it hung on for weeks. And then, of course, there was my brother's death . . ." His voice trailed off, and he just sat there looking very tired.

"It's like a row of dominoes," another member of the class said, and we all looked at the man with new compassion. The promotion had set off a tremor across the surface of his life, leading to inner reorientations that were hard for the man to put into words. His brother's unexpected death at forty-eight and his own illness combined to undermine his old sense of invulnerability. The firing of his friend had the same effect because it was not incompetence but organizational needs over which he had no control that had sent the man packing. "I've never felt this way before," the man said at the end of the evening, "but I feel as though my whole life was built on a frozen lake. We all go on with our activities. We work on the house and play golf and entertain and have our fights. I put in long hours at work and think I'm doing well. Then every once in a while I think, 'This is ice I'm standing on, and it's melting'—or 'Was that a crack I heard just then?' I try to forget, but I keep thinking, 'Damn, that ice looks thin!'"

This man was in a time of profound personal transition, one of those times of important realignment that punctuate everyone's life on occasion. Under the deceptively smooth surface of a good job and a comfortable home, he was fighting for his life. He wanted the promotion, but he longed for the easier life he had left behind. The change that put him into transition was one that anyone would have called "good," but it threatened to undermine his life as completely as death or disaster or any other "bad" change. The transition began at one place in his life, but its effects reached across every aspect of his world.

Few people stop to reflect, as this man had to, on the radiating waves of change in their lives. When they do, they may find that apparently minor events have had major impacts. They may find that puzzling and hard-to-identify distresses can be traced back to incidents that set off the transition process. Sometimes the distresses involve new beginnings that require unforeseen endings; sometimes they involve endings with no new beginning in sight. The big events—divorce, death, losing a job, and other obviously painful changes—are easy to spot. But others, such as marriage, sudden success, and moving to your dream house, are forgotten because they are "good events" and therefore not supposed to lead to difficulty. We expect to be distressed by illness, but it is a shock when recovery leads to difficulty. We know that overworking is hard, but how can a big vacation lay us low? And how shall we account for the puzzling chains of events, none of which are especially big or traumatic, that make our lives look like Rube Goldberg machines, one piece setting another into motion and the end result being way off in the corner somewhere. When a child enters school, a woman is free to take an outside job, and that additional money makes possible the first big vacation in years—at which time the husband decides to change jobs. The mechanics are not very elegant, but this is the way life works.

We'll move on shortly to ways of understanding these distresses and how they seem to cluster at certain times in the life cycle, but for now it is important for you to think as clearly as you can about your own life situation. What are the events that have brought change into your life in the past year? And what are the areas of your life in which the changes are evident? Here are some categories and guidelines to help you answer those questions.

Losses of relationships. What relationships have gone out of your life in the past year—list everything from a spouse's death to a friend's moving away. Include marital separations, children leaving home, or the alienation of a former friend. What about the death of a pet, or the loss of some admired hero, or anything that narrows your field of relationships?

Changes in home life. Getting married or having a child; having a spouse retire, becoming ill (or recovering), returning to school, changing jobs, or going into a depression; moving to a new house or remodeling the old one; experiencing increased (or decreased) domestic tension—anything that changed the content or quality of life in your home.

Personal Changes. Getting sick (or well again); experiencing notable success (or failure); changing your eating habits, sleep patterns, sexual activities; starting or stopping school; markedly changing your life-style or your appearance.

Work and financial changes. Getting fired, retiring, or changing jobs; changes within your organization; an increase or decrease in income; taking on new loans or mortgages; discovering that career advancement is blocked.

Inner changes. Spiritual awakening, deepening social and politi-
cal awareness, or psychological insights; changes in self-image or
values; the discovery of a new dream or the abandonment of an old
one; or simply one of those nameless shifts that cause us to say, "I'm
changing."

Two doctors named Thomas Holmes and Richard Rahe made
a list of these kinds of events and worked out a point system to
record the relative impact of each event on a person. The points
range from 100 for the death of a spouse to 11 for a minor violation
of the law. Hundreds of thousands of people have taken this test,
and their scores have been correlated with their health during the
ensuing year or two. The results are startling. A score of fewer than
150 points puts you in an "average" group, with one chance in
three of experiencing a serious health change in the next two years.
(On average, an American has a one-in-five chance of being hospi-
talized during this time.) If you score from 150 to 300 points, your
chances of health changes rise to fifty-fifty. And if you score more
than 300 points, as the man with the promotion unexpectedly did,
the odds for serious illness in the ensuing two years rise to almost
nine in ten.[3]

No wonder the man with the promotion got the virus! No wonder so many people find their situations complicated by illness
shortly after retirement. It makes you wonder about the frequency
of colds during honeymoons and realize that transition takes its toll
physically as well as mentally and socially.

It also makes you realize that there *are* times in everyone's life
that are transitional in more than a quantitative sense. Events pile
up outside us, and we respond inwardly in ways that leave us
changed. Not all transitions affect us deeply, of course, but some
endings do close entire chapters in our lives, and some beginnings

A Lifetime of Transitions

What animal walks on four feet in the morning, two feet at noon, and three feet in the evening, yet has only one voice?

—THE RIDDLE OF THE SPHINX

The human being.

—OEDIPUS'S SOLUTION TO THE RIDDLE

THE RIDDLE OF THE SPHINX WAS NO MERE TEST of wit, for it imparted valuable wisdom concerning how a person "stands" in the world. The riddle represents a model of the human lifetime in which there are two pivotal turning points. The first is the transition to the condition described in the phrase "standing on your own two feet"—that is, the transition from dependency to separateness and independence. The second turning point, coming somewhere in the afternoon of life, is symbolized by the acquisition of the cane or staff, the third foot of the Oedipal riddle. In the mythic story of Oedipus, the cane bespeaks not simply the coming of physical decrepitude but a cluster of changes that includes suffering and deepened insight and disengagement from an outlived way of doing and being.

Compared to our current theories of adult development, this image of the lifetime may seem simplistic. We miss Erikson's "identity crisis" in adolescence, and Sheehy's "trying twenties," Levinson's "settling down" in the thirties—and what about the notorious "mid-life crisis"? These ideas about adult development are all worth studying, but they do not invalidate the insight provided by the sphinx's riddle. The riddle reminds us that the lifetime can be thought of as having three natural phases and that each has its own characteristic style. Further, its context—the story of Oedipus—suggests that the transition from one phase to the next is difficult and involves certain problems.

In this chapter, we will look at these transitions in the context of a lifetime and the development that takes place at every stage of that journey. Only against that background does transition really make sense, for transition is simply the way in which one's life moves on and unfolds. The ending-then-beginning pattern represents the way a person changes and grows. And although it may be hard to think about larger issues while you are in the immediate turmoil of a transition, you must finally deal with them if you are to understand not only what is happening but why, when, and how it is happening. In other words, I am not telling you to stop bailing—just to cast an eye over the map and think about where your little boat is heading.

Neither of the transition points identified in the sphinx's riddle is likely to be negotiated in one event or period of change. The transition from dependency to independence, for example, usually includes gradually increasing degrees of separation between the individual and the parental world, as well as the various inner changes of values and identity by which the person develops a personal self-image and outlook. Nor is this process complete when you leave home or turn twenty-one: At thirty, forty, or even fifty, you are still likely to be making the changes that complete the great life-transition to personal independence.

But long before you have finished with that transition, you will begin to encounter the first signs of the second great life transition. "I can't be getting old yet!" exclaimed one of the men in the transition class, only half humorously. "I'm still struggling with my adolescence!" And we all knew how he felt. But nonetheless, sometime in your thirties, you are likely to note a shift in the wind that bespeaks a new weather system. The main storms are still well off beyond the horizon, but it is time to begin turning your attention away from the old issues of life's morning and toward those of its afternoon.

This theory, with its assertion of lifelong development and its claim that problems are often signals of life transitions, runs counter to modern mechanistic ideas about adulthood. Surrounded as we are by industrial products, we have tended to treat everything as if its essential nature were that of a product. In other words, we think of people as we think of cars; that is, as having times of production and function—and then, unfortunately, of falling apart.

This view of the lifetime, although it is outmoded, deserves a moment of our attention, for we need to understand its implications if we are not to fall back into it unwittingly. According to this view, human development is comparable to mechanical production—it begins when the item is not yet "done," and it ends when the item is ready to "use." Changes that occur after that point are "malfunctions" and signs that the mechanism needs repair. Whatever is done then involves finding some faulty part, just as the production process involved putting together the parts in the "right way." With cars, you start with the chassis, then add and assemble the motor and the other components, attach the outer body, and then paint it. And with people, we imagine, something similar goes on: first this training, and then that experience, and, finally, that influence, one after the other, all adding up to the finished person, twenty-one years old and ready to roll.

The idea that de-velop-ment (which means "unfolding") continues uninterruptedly throughout a lifetime is entirely foreign to the world of products. Think how strange it would be to have an automobile mechanic lift the hood of your car and say, "Hey, see that swelling on the side of the cylinder block? That's your second carburetor beginning to bud." Machines don't do that. VWs do not turn into Volvos when they are five years old, nor do they sprout a fifth gear at 45,000 miles. The rattle and clanking you hear are not a sign that an old transition is still being completed or that a new transition is beginning. They're simply a sign that something is wrong with the car and that it needs fixing.

We are beginning to understand that this production analogy has led to a serious misunderstanding of our real nature and that we need new ways of thinking about the life cycle. As soon as we realized this lack, various books on "adult development" appeared in the bookstores. The trend began in the early seventies with a few books on middle age, and then the floodgates were opened by Gail Sheehy's *Passages*. Subtitled *The Predictable Crises of Adult Life*, that book promised to make sense out of the changes we knew we were all experiencing. Then Sheehy's two main sources of research published their own books: Roger Gould came out with *Transformations: Growth and Change in the Adult Years*, and Daniel J. Levinson published *The Seasons of a Man's Life*. And now, thirty years later, as the enormous generation of boomers is entering middle age, a raft of books on aging have appeared. You would think that this previously uncharted second half of life would be pretty well mapped by now.

But there is still a good deal of confusion, for like those early maps of America, some of the explorers put the river here, some put it there, and some said there was no river. In other words, there is no shortage of theory—just considerable discrepancy between theorists. That's where the sphinx comes to our rescue, for when you start with the basic three-phase life image, you can draw on current theory to suggest different aspects of each phase and why a particular time of transition involves the particular issues that it does. In so doing, you can see that the force of life's two great developmental shifts fan out over the lifetime: The first involves an end to old dependencies and the establishment of the person as a separate social entity; the second involves movement beyond that separateness to something more complex, to a deeper sense of interrelatedness. The middle third of life is characterized by a mixture of these two influences. Although the particulars cannot be pinned down into a generally applicable chronology, you will be able to find the signs of them in your own life history.

Let's go back to a beginning before adulthood starts—the turning point at the end of childhood. Our culture is too individualistic to have standardized the experience, as most earlier cultures did, but you will experience unique associations to the phrase "the end of childhood."

The End of Chilhood. How does that phrase recall your past? Your first sexual experience, perhaps, or your family's move to a new town. You might date it from the beginning of a new interest or from the ending of an old relationship. Or you may associate it with a less clearcut change—no big event, no particular situation, just the sense, as you walked home alone from school or sat looking out of your bedroom window, that you weren't the same, that childhood had disappeared like yesterday's weather.

Tribal societies usually placed great emphasis on this transition point, as did ancient civilizations. They compressed the entire maturation process into one memorable event and used the occasion to dramatize and facilitate the transformation of a young person from dependency to independence. Furthermore, the coming-of-age rituals set the tone for a lifetime of subsequent transformations and their celebrations.

It's worth reflecting on this early transition in your own life because that point may have set the style for your later transitions. That happened with me, I think. At the end of grammar school, I happened to move from a very small town to a medium-sized city, and from a little school to a big one. My old friends had been unsophisticated kids, for the most part, and I felt at home with them. But then suddenly I was in school with children who paid attention to what they wore and who knew about city life and moved with the times. I had to change my way of life to fit in, and for some time I felt like a displaced person. It is probably no accident that I tend to view my own life transitions as shifts in lifestyle and to associate them with physical moves.

It was quite different for Joanna, a fortyish member of my first transition seminar. She had been separated from her husband for several months and was so immobilized by the change that she hardly spoke during the first weeks of the class. As she told us later, she was holding on to her past and refusing to start life anew as a single person. It was almost as if she didn't know how to let go, as if she were waiting for a signal.

Then one night in class she started to talk. A terrible thing had happened that week, she said. She had been driving along a winding road in the evening and, coming around a corner, she had been momentarily blinded by the lights of an oncoming car. Swerving to avoid it, she had run off the road.

The car had been badly damaged and she had been cut and bruised. But she had somehow also been set into motion, for in the next few days she had found a part-time job and had moved in with a friend to save money. And now she was beginning to talk to her classmates for the first time.

It was a terrible experience, she kept repeating. She might have killed that other driver. "I know what it does to a person to be responsible for somebody's death," she said, and she began to cry. "I saw what it did to my mother. It's an incredible coincidence, really, but when I was thirteen my whole world was changed by another automobile accident. My mother was driving us all to school one morning, and she didn't see a stoplight and ran into a big truck. My sister was very badly hurt, and I was out of school myself for a while."

We all sat there stunned, as much by her sudden volubility as by the coincidence of her misfortune. She went on to say that her mother had become very depressed after the accident and had, in effect, stopped taking care of the house. Joanna had to take over the responsibilities of cooking and cleaning. "I was forcibly evicted from childhood. That accident did it," she said.

Did Joanna contrive to reenact this terrible event to terminate another chapter in her life, we all wondered? Or did the ending that she needed to make remain unrealized until the right event brought it to the surface? There are no simple answers to these questions, and those two possibilities may not be mutually exclusive. The point is that Joanna and I (and quite possibly you) had a memorable transition experience around the end of childhood, and that experience was established in our awareness as a model for sub-sequent life transitions. Because we lack formal rites of passage and guidance in these matters, it is not surprising that the basic form of that experience or elements from it may reappear later in our lives.

The ending of childhood is one part of the shift from life's morn-ing (or dependence) to life's noon (or independence). A second part of that shift involves establishing a separate identity, distinct from that of being so-and-so's child. In traditional societies, the new identity was partly prescribed by your status and clan and partly dis-covered during the rite of passage, when some guardian spirit or an-cestor or guru gave you a new name and a new sense of destiny. With us, the old prescriptions have largely broken down, and we have fallen back on the idea that an identity is assembled during youth.

The psychologist Erik Erikson has explained how that process of identity formation works during youth, when a person tries on a se-ries of roles and experiments with different kinds of relationships.[1] Daughter, good athlete, average student, girlfriend, actress, sister, babysitter, pal, shy person, closet moralist, dreamer—out of this pot-pourri of identities some coherent sense of self must be formed. This is the developmental business of youth, says Erikson. He called it the *task* of this phase of life.

Every phase of life has such a task, and failing to complete it sat-isfactorily means that you make the transition into the next phase accompanied by unfinished business. And most of us didn't entirely finish the job of resolving identity issues back then. Consequently, whenever we enter a new transition, some of those old identity is-sues are going to reemerge. "I feel like I'm sixteen again," said a woman in the transition seminar. "The divorce took away the main identity I'd had for six years, and I find myself now trying out different ways of being, different roles, almost different personalities, the way I did when I was a teenager." This had been a disturbing experience for her, although after we talked about the way transition reactivates our old identity crises, she discovered that once she had accepted her experience as natural, she rather enjoyed it.

Each member of a tribal group moves straight from childhood into adulthood, but most modern people do not. Instead, in slowly changing forms, our dependency continues for some years. We eat the food our parents buy, we live in their house, we turn to them for help when we face some difficulty. But slowly all this changes, and then one day we are finally on our own. That is the next important transition point for most people: the time when they leave home and set up shop for themselves.

On Your Own: What memories and feelings do you associate with that phrase? You may think of moving into an apartment with several friends and getting your first real job, or you may think of a series of gradual shifts—going away to school (but remaining financially dependent); taking a part time job (but having to borrow money from your parents for graduate school); and, finally, finishing school and earning enough to settle your debts with your parents. Some people react sadly to thinking about being on their own: "I don't think I really made that transition," said a woman in that first transition seminar. "Here I am at fifty, with my children flying the coop, and I'm only now beginning to taste what it's like to be on your own. I got married so fast after I left home that I just switched dependencies."

People's experiences vary greatly here. Charles Dickens was hardly more than ten when he went to work in a London blacking factory and lived by his wits in a nearby slum. No unfinished business there—except that the insecurities created by this premature independence stayed with Dickens all his life. At the other extreme, I knew a man of seventy who lived with his parents and worked for his ninety-five-year-old father in the family business. No insecurities for him—that is, so long as he kept his life within the tiny circle of his familiar childhood world and excluded alien experiences, such as mature relationships and a real career. Those are extreme examples, of course, but most of us can find in our lives some vestige of the transition to living on our own.

What comes next in this ongoing transformation of the dependent child into independent adult? As the initial excitement and panic of being separate from the parental orbit begin to wane, new questions arise, and the emphasis shifts from leaving something to finding and fitting into something else. This is what Daniel J. Levinson calls the phase of "entering the adult world."[2] Erikson says that the major developmental task at that time is forging strong new interpersonal relationships and thereby exploring your capacity for intimacy. In the broadest sense, we might say that this time is one of "searching for a place" and that the transitions likely to take place involve experimenting with an eye to making commitments.

Some people move quickly at this time. They marry, launch careers, and begin families. They find a place for themselves fast and make long-range commitments, but with little experimenting. Others hang back, trying out various relationships, various jobs, and several different living situations. They leave school to work for a while, and then return to school after taking some time off to do nothing but travel. For these people, the search for their place in the world involves dozens of transitions spread out over ten years, but for others, all the transitionality is compressed into one grand leap into marriage and a career.

In pointing out this contrast, I am not saying that one way is better than the other. I only suggest that even diverse life experiences reflect the same basic transitional task of shifting from the centrifugal force of leaving childhood to the centripetal one of finding a suitable place in the world. There is no right way, for every way has its price and its rewards. The early place finders may later regret that they did not try different options before making long-term commitments, and the experimenters may wonder whether they waited too long and missed some hidden moment when settling down would have felt just right and would have worked. Both groups tend to find themselves asking these questions as they approach thirty. Levinson calls this time the "age thirty transition"; Gould emphasizes a growing realism about oneself and calls it a time of "opening up to what's inside."[3] Either way, the approaching thirtieth birthday seems to inspire second thoughts.

This can be the pivotal transitional point in a lifetime. Whatever it was that people were doing before begins to seem not quite right. About a third of the participants in that first transition seminar was within two or three years of thirty, and, even though they had initially failed to see what else they had in common, they were struck with this coincidence. Anne was getting a divorce, and Mort announced that he was at last preparing to settle down. Some people had just discovered meaningful work for the first time; others were ready to chuck good careers that they had worked hard to launch. Sally, aged thirty-four, was starting to think about how much longer she could safely wait to have her first child—and whether she really wanted children; Pat was almost ready to let her former husband take full custody of their child so that she could resume the career that she had left to get married. The variety was immense. But beneath the surface, the various transitions began with the discovery that roles and relationships were starting to pinch and bind.

"I can't even remember how I got into this damned job," said Tod with disgust to the rest of the class one evening. "I went to graduate school to try to accomplish something and make a difference in the world, and here I am pushing papers all day, filling out forms that a high school kid could do. And the people at work! They don't even know who I am—or care."

Jannine listened to this with a puzzled look. "This all sounds strange to me because I've been envying your stability and security ever since our class began. I keep thinking, 'When does the Great Search end? Am I going to end up an old woman who lives with her cats and who's never stayed in one place more than two years?' I can hardly go through a residential neighborhood any more without wanting a house of my own so badly that I go home and start counting my assets again. I'm tired of the quest and the adventure."

Second thoughts can turn one's thirties into a difficult time. It is often the first time of transition after leaving home when a person feels real doubt about the future. It can also be a very lonely time, because the very people that one would normally talk to about personal problems may be the people that one is having second thoughts about. And the distress is deepened by that twisted old idea that if you'd only done things properly, you would have everything settled once and for all by twenty-five or so.

This transitionality around thirty was first noted seventy-five years ago by the Viennese psychologist Charlotte Buhler. In her study of hundreds of biographies, she found that although physical dependence on parents usually ended in the late teens, a successful and long-lasting set of commitments was usually not made until a person was almost thirty. The intervening years were likely to be spent in roles and relationships that were technically "adult" but were actually "preparatory [in] character" to what the person was going to do and be during the bulk of the adult years.[4]

Levinson's research on the lives of contemporary men and women suggests a similar finding, and he calls the years from twenty-two to thirty-three the "novice period" of adulthood. Perhaps it would be better if we viewed thirty rather than twenty-one as the first great watershed of the lifetime; or, better yet, if we viewed the end of childhood, the time of being on one's own, the search for a place and the time of second thoughts, as a series of times during which transitions accomplish the larger developmental business of transforming us from dependency to independence.

Throughout this novice period, transitions have a special poignancy and anxiousness about them, for they seem to threaten a return to the old dependency that we're trying to put behind us. Although it is only a move to a new town or a new job or the breaking up of a short-lived relationship, you feel as if you were going back to "Go." "I have to start all over," said a thirty-year-old businessman-turned-teacher, "and I feel like I missed the first hour of the race. I'm going to have to run like hell to catch up." "You think *you've* had a setback," muttered a man in the class who had married at eighteen and was now, at twenty-eight, in the midst of a trial separation. "Hell, I feel like I'm still a teenager, and the next thing I know I'll start taking my laundry home to Mom again!"

It's important to recognize the reason for these feelings and to realize that they are natural. Just because things are up in the air now and you sometimes feel as if you were right back where you started, this is not a sign that you have made a mistake or have been wasting your time for the past ten years. It is only a sign that you are in one of life's natural and periodic times of readjustment and renewed commitment. You are at the end of the novice period of adulthood, a time when long-term commitments are often made. You know the rules now, and you're beginning to sense what you can and cannot do well. They no longer ask to see your driver's license when you order a glass of wine. You are, for better or for worse, an undisputed grown-up. The question is, *now* what are you going to do?

How you handle the transitions that are prompted by second thoughts can determine the course of your life for years to come. Having decided to repress inner promptings to change, some people begin at this point to turn away from the opportunities for development provided by transition and instead deal with the times of transition as temporary and accidental disruptions in an otherwise stable life. In the short run, these people seem to gain by avoiding the time-consuming shifts and inner reorientation that others are going through; but in the long run, they lose. They turn into the brittle beauties of the suburbs and the company yes-men who rejoin them at the end of the day.

But for many others, this time of second thoughts provides a clearer sense of personal direction than they have hitherto known—and even some goal or project that embodies that direction. The thirties can be a time of new or renewed commitment to what Levinson calls "the tribe," some social grouping that has particular importance for the individual. This can be a formal organization or a profession, the community where one lives or an ethnic population of which one is a part, or "men" or "women" or "the working class," or even "humankind." Although he is writing only about men, Levinson's words apply to both sexes: After the "age thirty transition" comes a time for a man to join the tribe as a full adult on terms he can accept: time to find his niche, get plugged into society with greater commitment and responsibility, raise a family and exercise an occupation and do his bit for the survival and well-being of the tribe. . . . [Whatever the person's particular "tribe,"] everyone during Settling Down is strongly connected to a segment of his society, responsive to its demands and seeking the affirmation and rewards it offers.[5]

This "settling down" can represent a major life transition if the person has remained transient through the novice phase of adulthood, although for people who keep their initial relationships and work-life intact, it can mean no more than a slight reorientation and a renewed commitment after a time of reappraisal. I have the impression from the people whom I have worked with that those who tailor their situations to their own capacities and needs most carefully at this time make the most successful long-term commitments and that those who power their way through these shoals without much change are the ones who are heading for really rough times around forty. Be that as it may, this transition point sets the tone for much that follows in the middle decades of the lifetime.

It has been fashionable to highlight the next point of transition, to make it into the very center of the developmental design. Sometime around forty, so runs this argument, the skies darken and the seas rise and the crew casts worried glances toward the lifeboats. All ships head into the wind and prepare to ride out the most infamous of transitions: the mid-life crisis. (Sturm und Drang music, please.)

I used to subscribe to this theory. I was just turning forty and in the midst of the changes that led to the first transition seminar during which I tried to make sense out of "adult development." But thirty years later, I see matters differently.

The most important fact is not that there are one or three or four or six identifiable periods of crisis in a lifetime; rather, adulthood unfolds its promise in an alternating rhythm of expansion and contraction, change and stability. In human life as in the rest of nature, change accumulates slowly and almost invisibly until it is made manifest in the sudden form of fledging out or thawing or leaf-fall. It is the transition process rather than a thing called "a mid-life transition" that we must understand.

The second fact to remember is that, at forty, not everyone finds life coming to a halt or standing on its head. Rather, from the early thirties on, most people find life moving in alternating periods of stability and change. The mid-life transition is the first of these transition times after the end of the novice period, and for many people it is a time of considerable upheaval. But not everyone makes the biggest changes then. "I'm having my mid-life crisis at fifty-five," Tom kept reminding us during the transition seminar. "I may be a little slow," he'd say while leaning back in his chair, "but when I got there, I finally really let go!" (He had suddenly sold his furniture store the year before, and was now "into consciousness," whatever that meant.)

Another reason it is misleading to single out the mid-life transition for such special treatment is that it is the result not just of new factors but of a mixture of old and new ones. On the one hand, things are full of promise; on the other, they lack meaning. On the one hand, the kids are almost grown; on the other, the parents are getting old. On the one hand, forty is the beginning; on the other, it's the end.

"It's the mirror that does it to you first, I think," said Betty on one of the final nights of the seminar. "I still thought of myself as I had been ten years earlier, but one day I looked in the mirror and said, 'Where'd you come from, old gal? What ever happened to Betty—the girl that used to live here?'"

Within organizations, you may begin to notice a widening gap between you at forty and the younger employees. It is as though some unmarked boundary had been crossed unawares, and you are now in another country. The young and the old seem to have their own places in the structure, but the middle-aged have lost a sense of belonging.

It is no accident that such people should be ripe for a reassessment of the hopes and plans that brought them this far. Now is the time when the melancholy wit of Oscar Wilde hits home: "The Gods have two ways of dealing harshly with us—the first is to deny us our dreams, and the second is to grant them." If you've realized your dreams, you ask yourself, "Is this *it*? Is *this* what I've been trying to reach?" And if you've failed to realize them (and it tends to be around this time that such discoveries are made), you have to face what the existential psychologist James Bugental has called "the nevers": "I guess that I'm never going to be the head of the firm . . . never going to have children of my own . . . never going to be a great writer . . . never going to be rich . . . never going to be famous." For many, this is the time of coming to terms with the recognition that they have been chasing a carrot on a stick.

These discoveries are thought provoking, to say the least, but they sometimes open the door to new activities and new achievements that were impossible when you were under the spell of the old dreams. Carried free of the old conflicts and confusions of trying to make it, and carried out into the clear water of self-knowledge and service, many people find at last what they were meant to do and to be. Gandhi discovered at fifty his real mission in nonviolent resistance. Cervantes was older than that when he began his career as a novelist. Lou Andreas Salome was in her sixties when she became a psychoanalyst. And then there is Grandma Moses, not to mention Colonel Sanders.[6]

Some books offer roadmaps to the middle and later years by telling you what you ought to be doing when—or more likely, making you feel inadequate for not doing at fifty or seventy what they say you ought to be doing. But I think that is misleading; the whole idea of typical stages begins to break down as one enters the middle years. It is the business of constructing a separate and independent life that has stages, with first this and then that. The process of letting go of that style of living and discovering a different relation to things cannot so easily be reduced to fixed sequences. One has a sense of change, as with the weather towards the end of a season, but there seems to be no clear pattern, any more than there is with fall storms.

The transitions during this period depend less often on personal initiative and more often on someone else's actions, such as your child's decision to leave home or to marry. As you grow older, the illnesses and deaths among contemporaries carry with them the potential for unforeseen and unwanted transition. Yet every transition is an ending that prepares the ground for new growth and new activities.

As life passes, the second great point of transformation into the time in which the sphinx's image of the man with the staff is the dominant one, your own expectations become important. These are largely the product of your culture and family history. In the Orient, old age is revered as life's apex—a time of greatest influence and deepest wisdom. The ancient Hindu image of the lifetime has an important transition point around the time of the birth of one's grandchildren. Until that time, one has been in the *House-holder* stage of life, a time in which self-fulfillment and personal development have involved participating in social roles, family life, and the world of work. But now you are ready for a change—a change caught in the very name of the next life stage, that of the *Forest-Dweller.*

This important life transition, for which we in the West have no real name or concept, comes when, in the words of religious historian Huston Smith,

> the time has come for the individual to begin his true adult education, to discover who he is and what life is all about. What is the secret of the "I" with which he has been on such intimate terms all these years, yet which remains a stranger? What lurks behind the world's façade, animating it, ordering it—to what end?[7]

As the Hindu name of this life stage suggests, the transition into it is one of turning away from the world's business and going into the solitude of the forest for a time of reflection and study.

This in an important shift during life's second half, which is not the same as our retirement because it is a transition *into* something, not just a transition *from* something. Whether or not we acknowledge it, this transition corresponds to inward changes that are evident in many Americans' lives. It is marked by a growing concern for the significance and meaning of what has been done as well as a loss of interest in simple success. One of the members of the transition class put it this way: "I took an early retirement, although it wasn't for the leisure as such that I did it. The idea of sitting on the beach or puttering in the garden doesn't appeal to me much, but I wanted to use the time to . . . well, think. That sounds funny, I guess. I never was any great brain, and I was so busy selling that I never read very much. But still, even though I can't exactly say why, I really want time to think now." Several of the older class members nodded in recognition.

This shift was common among the middle-aged and older patients of the Swiss psychiatrist Carl Jung. Describing the typical outlook of such a patient, Jung wrote:

> Social usefulness is no longer an aim for him, although he does not question its desirability. Fully aware as he is of the social unimportance of his creative activity, he looks upon it as a way of working out his own development.[8]

The developmental process at this point seems to be akin to ripening. No wonder it has failed to show up on the measures of external change—except in a negative sense as a loss of interest in external achievement.

The transitions of life's afternoon are more mysterious than those of its morning, and so we have tended to pass them off as the effects of physical aging. But something deeper is going on, something as purposive in its own way as the development of social roles and interpersonal relationships in life's first half. The loss of interest in the accomplishments that motivated your life's first half is matched by a growth of interest in psychological and spiritual matters.

There exists a great myth that portrays this shift from life's morning to its afternoon, the change from two-leggedness to three. That is the myth of Odysseus, the Greek hero of the Trojan War. He is older than many of the other warriors, a middle-aged married man and the father of a nearly grown son back on the island of Ithaca. On a literal level, the tale that bears his name tells about the mysterious setbacks that cause his three-week homeward voyage to become a ten-year journey; but on a deeper level, it tells about another kind of journey. This is no simple "trip," but rather the journey of personal transformation that becomes possible after you have done the world's business for long enough. Because *The Odyssey* tells so memorably about this homing process, it is worth reviewing.

The story begins with difficulties. As Odysseus explains to anyone who will listen, the problems involve a terrible and unexpected defeat right after the enormous victory at Troy. Odysseus and twelve shiploads of men had put ashore at the village of Ismaros. They wanted just a little more loot and some wine for the trip home. To these brave victors from the plains of Troy, Ismaros looked like a pushover. But something happened. The soldiers took too long and drank too much; a neighboring tribe rode out of the hills and caught them unawares, and these great warriors were sent limping back to their ships, beaten and wounded.

What had happened? What had gone wrong? This was the sort of thing that Odysseus had become famous for doing well—but now the strategy had failed. The incident at Ismaros sets the tone for *The Odyssey*, for throughout the tale Odysseus discovers in one way and then another that he has crossed some mysterious line in his life and that everything that once worked for him now works against him. Like most of us, Odysseus is a slow learner—or unlearner, for it turns out that his most difficult tasks are those of unlearning much that brought him to life's middle years and to the height of his renown.

Consider Odysseus's attempt to sail safely between Scylla and Charybdis, the monster and the whirlpool that have come to stand in the Western imagination for the impossible choices in life. The sorceress Circe had explained to him that he could negotiate the narrows only if he did not resist the dangers there. Odysseus demurred, announcing that he was Odysseus and would never turn away from combat. "You rash man," she replied. "Do the works of war concern you still, and toil? Will you not yield to the immortal gods?" But when he arrived at the narrow place in the journey, he "forgot the hard injunction of Circe, when she ordered me in no way to arm myself. I put on my famous armor, took two long spears in my hands, and went up on the deck of the ship at the prow." The little man standing on the deck of a fragile vessel, playing the hero when the time for heroism had passed!

It is significant that, here, as elsewhere in the epic, Odysseus's help and insights came from women. In *The Iliad*, of course, everything had been male, but in *The Odyssey* it is to the wisdom of the opposite sex that our hero must turn to find the way. It is no accident, of course, that Odysseus's journey home is toward his feminine counterpart, Penelope. In symbolic terms, he is coming home to his own feminine side.

Poor Penelope, weaving and unweaving her cloth while the hundred suitors propositioned her and ate and drank everything in the house. If this were her story, you can bet it would have been different. At forty, she would probably have told everyone what they could do with that drafty old palace, and she might have had a fling with one of the suitors, too. She would have done her own "exploring," just as Odysseus had done, and would have found much to learn from mentors of the opposite sex.

The point is that in life's second-half task of "homecoming," your encounters with the powers of the opposite sex are symbolic in a way that is different from life's first half. Carl Jung emphasized the same point:

> We might compare masculinity and femininity . . . to a particular store of substances of which, in the first half of life, unequal use is made. A man consumes his large supply of masculine substance and has left over only the smaller amount of feminine substance, which he must now put to use. It is the other way round with a woman; she allows her unused supply of masculinity to become active.[9]

Odysseus literally goes through hell on his way home—as most of us do. His visit is made in a different spirit from those underworld journeys taken by younger mythic heroes. His is not an exploit or a test of his manhood, for Odysseus journeys into hell humbly and because it is a necessary part of his homecoming. We all go through hell to learn what we need to learn to complete our life's journey.

By the time of his hell-visit, Odysseus has lost much of his brittle pride. His homeward journey has been marked by a process of constant attrition. He started with twelve ships, then six were destroyed, and later three more. Finally, he was down to one, manned by the few men who were left with him. And at the end he was alone, his last boat sucked down and ripped apart in the great whirlpool of Charybdis. Metaphorically, he is stripped of the various supports on which he had earlier relied. As grievous as that loss is, it also leaves him able to know himself in a new sense.

In suffering this attrition, Odysseus discovers a kind of courage that is different from the cunning and the aggressiveness of the battlefield. That courage is manifested when his boat is caught in the whirlpool. Just as it is being sucked down to destruction, he reaches up and grabs the branch of a fig tree that hangs over the water. With a new kind of bravery, he holds on, not knowing whether it will really matter, until suddenly the whirlpool regurgitates all that is left of his ship: the naked keel and the bare mast. Letting go at last of his painful hold, Odysseus drops athwart the keel and paddles with his hands out to sea. This king and hero, who began with a fleet of ships, leaves the scene like a child astride a log.

This same stripping-down process characterizes Odysseus's earlier encounter with the giant Polyphemus, who returns unexpectedly to find Odysseus and his men exploring the cave where he lives. Blocking the entrance with immense boulders, Polyphemus traps the warriors and begins eating them, two at a meal. Nevertheless, through ingenuity, Odysseus and his remaining troops soon manage to get free.

When Polyphemus discovers their escape, he calls to his neighboring giants for help, shouting that "Oudeis" has escaped. *Oudeis*, which was what Odysseus had called himself when he met the giant, is the Greek word for "nobody." So when Polyphemus shouts that nobody has injured him and that nobody is escaping, the other giants simply shake their heads and wonder what is wrong with their friend.

In the world of Greek heroes, Odysseus has just done a unique thing: He has given up his identity. Identities meant fame, and fame meant power. Great heroes sometimes won combats simply by scaring off their opponents. "I am Heracles . . . Achilles . . . the great Theseus." To say, "I am Nobody" and to find in that new nonidentity a source of power—that is something significant, and it marks a stage of development going beyond the reliance on roles and the "standing-on-my-own-two-feet" stance that is natural to life's mid-day. (It is also no accident that the giant who opposes Odysseus in this initiatory struggle carries the name *Polyphemus,* meaning "famous" in Greek.) For Odysseus has reached the point in his development where he must begin to turn back on himself those forces he has been directing outward at the world. It is the point at which the hero must stop slaying dragons and begin slaying the dragonslayer.

Throughout Odysseus's long journey home, he is confronted by one distraction after another, each of which has its meaning in the context of life's second half. There is the song of the Sirens, which symbolizes the self-destruction lurking beneath the beguiling surface of all that calls upon us to turn aside. There is the lotus fruit, which stands for all that makes us forget the journey itself and our real destination. There is Calypso's promise: "Stay with me and you need never grow old." That fantasy—that we can stop the on-going process of life transitions—represents the most tempting and illusory promise of all. In spite of lapses, Odysseus somehow struggles past each blandishment as he struggled through the batterings.

Odysseus has not overcome all the difficulties when he finally lands in Ithaca. Things are a mess at home. The rival princes are overrunning his palace, living off his riches, and usurping his rightful place. At the mythic level, these interlopers correspond to all the inner confusions and distractions that block our inner homecomings—all those usurpers that move in to run things whenever our awareness absents itself. Just as we are about to reclaim the inner kingdom of selfhood, home at last from the long journey, we discover not only that there is no welcoming committee on the dock to meet us but that we must fight our way into our own rightful place. So in the end, the homeward journey of life's second half demands three things: First, that we unlearn the style of mastering the world that we used to take us through the first half of life; second, that we resist our own longings to abandon the developmental journey and refuse the invitations to stay forever at some attractive stopping place; and third, that we recognize that it will take real effort to regain the inner "home."

The Odyssey is an important corrective to the view that most of us grew up with: that the years between thirty and sixty form an unbroken plain, and that people do not change significantly from the time they become situated to the time they retire. So, too, are the careers of those individuals who broke the unwritten rule that after forty it is all replay. Consider Joshua Slocum, who set out at fifty-one to sail around the world alone and made it three years later. And Handel, who was deeply in debt and struggling to recover from a stroke when he accepted at fifty-seven a commission to write a choral work for a charitable performance and produced the *Messiah*. And Edith Hamilton, who did not even begin her work as a mythographer until after she retired from teaching at sixty—and who inaugurated at ninety a series of four annual trips to Europe.[10]

The transitions in life's second half offer a special kind of opportunity to break with the social conditioning that has carried us successfully this far and to do something really new and different. It is a season more in tune than the earlier ones with the deeper promptings of the spirit.

Unfortunately, it is also a time when we are surrounded by distractions. We're often still actively involved with our careers, and the house may not be paid for—oh, yes, and the kids aren't done with college, and all our security is tied up in the company's pension plan. Maybe we're coping with menopause or struggling across the burning sands of middle age. This is a hell of a bad time to start talking about new beginnings!

Perhaps. Certainly I'm not trying to provide another kind of pre-scription—a new change that we are all supposed to go through in unison at forty-five or sixty-five. I simply want to argue that the path of aging is not a downward slope, and that it is a unique journey for everyone who takes it. The truth is that, although ours is a youth-oriented culture, many of us do not come into our own until our lives are half or three-quarters over. Schopenhauer noted this more than a century ago, writing that each person's "character seems best suited to one particular stage of life; so that he appears at his best in that stage of life."[11]

This suggests that whatever else transition may give to or take away from our lives, it leads us at some point into our own best time of life. How has it been for you? What would you say is your own natural stage of life? Were you born to be seventeen or seventy? Are you a perennial twenty-five-year-old, or are you still waiting for your entrance cue at fifty? One often hears evidence about these matters in discussions of which birthdays are hardest. There is always dis-agreement, for what is really being discussed is when some self-image went out of sync with the calendar. What has your own expe-rience with this been?

Expand this recollection a little. Which of your own life transi-tion points have been the most important so far? We have been dis-cussing a series of typical times of transition and the developmental issues that are critical at each stage. But forget that. What is the chronology of your own experience with transition? Begin with the end of childhood and move up to the present. In some of these tran-sitions, nothing very important changed. But in others, a chapter of your life ended. Make a list of these significant transitions.

When you have done this, begin with the early transitions and see what you can say about the "developmental issues" that were involved in each transition. Here are some of the entries I made when I did this:

1951 — 17 years old: entered college; first time on my own; first real test of my abilities.

1955 — 21 years old: graduation; panic over career; decide to stay in school and avoid moment of decision; change of universities, but real transition avoided.

1956 — 22 years old; drafted into army; sudden entry into "the real world"; freedom from old expectations and self-image.

1958 — 24 years old: discharged; grappling again with the question of career.

And so on. Your chronology and the transitional events may be more decisive than mine were. Obviously, I found it very hard to get going on a career, and several of my transitions back then represented false starts.

An interesting sidelight on your own course of life can be found if you compare your chronology with that of the parent of your sex. Many of your life expectations come from the model provided for you by that parent. Although it will not show up on a developmental scheme, the age at which your parent dies (especially if it is early) will probably be an important point in your own life history. So can the point at which a parent's life came together to become interesting and productive, or the point at which things seemed to fall apart or go dead. What about the point at which your parent developed a serious illness or the point at which your parents divorced or the time that a parent changed the course of his or her life?

Comparing your chronology with that of your parents, you will come across milestones and detour markers that you scarcely noticed before. One of the men in the transition seminar discovered somewhat unexpectedly that he had quit his job at approximately the same age that his father had made a similar change twenty-five years earlier. "Am I copying him?" he asked, puzzled. "I hope not, because that decision was a terrible mistake for my father—he never found a really good job again after that." Another member of the class found close parallels between changes in her health and those of her mother, changes that had had a great impact on her as a girl. Still another class member had refused to retire at the usual time, not because he liked his work or because he needed the salary, but because his father had been miserable from the moment he retired.

It is important to identify those transition points that simply correspond to transitions your parents made, since these points represent programming that may have nothing to do with the realities in your own life. In the same way, it is important to clarify how much of what you experience during a time of transition is actually yours and how much is a cultural overlay—fifty-year-olds are supposed to feel thus-and-so. Even the current theories about adult life can become a substitute for a real awareness of what is actually happening to you. For ultimately each of us is on a unique journey with a ticket marked "Good for this trip only—no transfers."

Nonetheless, there are developmental issues that we all deal with at some point along the way. The sphinx's riddle suggests the two most important ones—the first being the transition by which a dependent creature moves into a separate independence and develops a self-image and a personal style. And then later, the same self-image and personal style hinder growth, and the person must face

3

Relationships and Transition

It takes a long time to be really married. One marries many times at many levels within a marriage. If you have more marriages than you have divorces within the marriage, you're lucky and you stick it out.

—**RUBY DEE**
In Brian Lanker, I Dream a World[1]

People change and forget to tell each other.

—**LILLIAN HELLMAN,**
Toys in the Attic[2]

LET'S BEGIN WITH AN IMAGINARY FAMILY. DON, aged forty-one, is a teacher at the local high school; he's been there for twelve years and is growing bored with the place, with teaching, with teenagers—even with himself. Betty, aged thirty-nine, was a teacher, too, before their children were born, but she hasn't done anything but part-time work outside the home for fifteen years. Now, however, she is talking about returning to school to earn a counseling license and launch a new career. Susan, aged sixteen, is a high school junior who is beginning to think about college; she is very bright and socially active, but is so busy that it seems she sometimes comes home only to change clothes and to sleep. Bob, aged fifteen, is equally bright but much shyer and less busy; he's a whiz at math and science and talks about a career in electrical engineering or aircraft design.

The stereotypical "happy, successful family" in many ways, especially when portrayed in this snapshot fashion. But they are really people in motion, and the snapshot cannot show that. Don, for example, is really distressed with his life these days. Sometimes, when the problem seems to be just the job, he thinks that if he finds something more interesting to do, everything will be better. But at other times, he doubts that the answer can be so simple. He and Betty are arguing more than they ever have before—about her plans and their impact on the family, about his moodiness and lack of interest in anything. "I need a change. That's all," he says. But it sounds hollow, even to him.

In fact, his life has come to a standstill. He feels empty and lost. He looks at Betty across the table or the bedcovers and tries to remember the old attraction he felt for her. A nice person, certainly; quick and warm. How can he *not* find her attractive? Other men do. He noticed that at the party the other night. Not that she was leading them on—just that all evening she was talking to men, and he could see that they found her attractive. So why didn't he?

After the party, they had come home and made love. Still excited by the evening, Betty was alive and responsive, and that turned him on. But only initially. After a little while, he lost his erection and they had to stop. This made Betty angry, and she wanted to know what was wrong. Nothing, nothing was wrong. This made her angrier, and she said harsh things about his being distant and cold. "You never used to be like this," she said. "What's happening to you?"

Don fought back, of course, but later, lying awake long after Betty had fallen asleep, her words echoed in his head. She was right. He never used to be like this. He thought of Pete, his lawyer and good friend, who had just left his family and moved into a city apartment. *He* had been bored, too. *He* had had trouble with sex, too. And now *he* had a whole new life, including fantastic sex again—at least, that's what he said. Maybe marriages have only so much shelf life; maybe they're only made to go 100,000 miles, or maybe you're supposed to get a new one every fifteen years. Perhaps this was just some natural end point that is built into relationships; maybe it's only fear and guilt that holds you in place after you come to that end point.

Dilemmas like these can plague younger couples, too. Don and Betty's marriage had seen such dilemmas ten or twelve years earlier, but at that time things hadn't seemed so serious. They had been married for only five or six years, the kids were young, and Don was just about to move to his present job. He remembered feeling dissatisfied then, too. Betty had not been very responsive sexually and they never seemed to go anywhere or do anything interesting. But then the job at the new school had come to his rescue. Betty and the kids liked the new house, and everything seemed to have blown over. They were so busy and involved that their underlying responses to that earlier transition were never even put into words. But now . . . would it blow over again?

That wasn't a question that could easily be answered because it depended not only on Don but on Betty and what she wanted out of life. When they had moved into their house, she had been tied down by two little children. "The other adults I see all day," she used to say to Don, "are other trapped mothers, retired people, and the clerks at Safeway. *You* get to see the world." Although she was often unhappy then, she saw no alternative. And worse, she suspected that if she thrashed around too much, Don, who seemed restless himself, might start looking for someone less bitchy and difficult.

But now things were different. Not that she wanted to leave the marriage; it was just that she no longer felt trapped in the old way. The children were almost on their own now, and she had her new dream of a counseling career. She no longer had to accept an impossible situation. The long and lonely years of early parenthood were behind her, and she felt a new excitement at the thought of moving out and finding a separate place for herself in the world.

Yet the situation scared her, too, for the better she felt about herself, the worse Don seemed to feel about himself. There seemed to be energy for only one of them within their relationship, and the more she had, the less he had. His loss of interest in sex was an example. The other night was the worst, but it had been heading in that direction for some time. He always used to take the initiative sexually, often urging her to try things that she felt shy about trying, or wanting to have sex when she really wasn't very interested. But now it was she, more often than not, who took the initiative. And it was she who seemed to enjoy sex more than he did. She was now more interested in sex and more responsive than she had been at thirty. She and Don were both changing, but changing, it seemed, in opposite directions. In time, she thought, they could have moved so far apart that they would be out of sight of each other.

It might be better if they separated. Maybe they were no longer good for each other. Certainly he was a drain on her energy and he often felt like a dead weight that she had to lug around—like the other night at the party. Out of the corner of her eye, she saw him looking at her all night long as she talked and laughed with others.

It was worse when she talked with men and felt enlivened by their interest in her. That was fun, and she had to admit that it made her realize that if she ever did leave Don, she needn't resign herself to isolation and celibacy.

But the sexual thing was really secondary, she thought. The primary thing was her new sense of purpose and the readiness she felt to meet the world head-on. She was ready to *do* things, and she hadn't felt that way since she graduated from college. The only problem was, could she continue to feel this way around Don? Would she have to choose between checking her own momentum and leaving him behind? She could suggest (and not for the first time) that he see a psychotherapist, but he would just say, "That's your old counselor number again, Betty. I'll handle this my way." Would this all just blow over, or might she have to do something?

The answer to that question hinges on what you mean by "blow over." If you mean the particulars—the fight last night and today's tensions—then the answer may well be *yes*. The old ups and downs will be replaced by new ups and downs. But if you mean the changes going on within Betty and Don and the transition their relationship is consequently going through, then the answer is probably *no*. For changes that are so deep and far-reaching are unlikely to disappear with time.

Each of these individuals is coming to the point where their separate, personal transitions are having an impact on their relationship. Having come to the end of a phase of their individual lives, they are finding that the relationship that served them pretty well up to this point is being put under enormous strain. The sexual difficulties are just the tip of the iceberg, and a repair job there will simply transfer the difficulty to a new area. Communication is terribly important, but improving how they talk to one another will achieve much less than will finding out what they really want to say to each other when they do talk. And, yes, roles need to be renegotiated, too, but not until these people go through their transitions and see what their "new" lives consist of can they arrive at an enduring arrangement.

You have probably already realized that neither Don nor Betty gave themselves room to deal with any of the *second thoughts* that had surfaced ten years earlier. Back then, they felt that they couldn't afford to take the time; and then a new external situation came along to distract them, so they didn't have to. In fact, Don had been unhappy with teaching then and had begun to realize that he had originally gravitated toward that kind of work only because he had always liked school and didn't know what else to do. The new job, together with a new home in a new community, made him forget his doubts and his longing for a deeper kind of new beginning.

The same thing had happened with Betty. The product of a very traditional upbringing, she had never really asked herself whether she wanted children right away. In spite of having just taken a job, she became pregnant and "had to" leave her career. She didn't experience herself as making conscious choices—or even having the freedom to do so.

Neither Betty nor Don had changed much between the ages of twenty and thirty-five, although from that point on both of them found it more and more difficult to summon the energy necessary to do the old things in the old way. But their situations were different. Betty could look forward to a built-in ending in a few years, brought on by the children's increasing independence and their launch into separate lives. As they grew older, they needed their mother less and less, and Betty's original desire for a career was renewed.

But Don had no built-in ending—not, at least, until retirement, and he certainly couldn't wait that long for relief. Nor was leaving teaching really the issue at this point, for the onerous responsibility of work that he did not like was only a symptom of a deeper difficulty. Having been a stranger to his own real needs and interests for so long, he no longer knew what he wanted, or even who he was. "I feel like I left myself a thousand miles back, somewhere," he said later when he and Betty went together to talk with a counselor. "The train just went on and on until finally it ran out of fuel and stopped, and then I couldn't pretend any longer that everything was OK."

Don's problem—whether you take that to be impotence or boredom with work or loss of interest in marriage—was not the important thing, and attempts to solve the problem outside the context of their lives as a whole would have provided no solution. It would have been like fueling up the train again and sending it farther down the track into the wilderness. The *problem* was simply a signal that the time had come to stop something—not to stop teaching or to end the marriage or to cease making love, but rather to recognize a less literal "end of the line" when they reached it.

For Don, this recognition led to some far-reaching changes over the next several years. After the first impulses to leave his career and his marriage, he decided to stay with both. He and Betty worked out a time plan for the next two years; after that, she would be working and earning enough money to take some of the pressure off Don and give him room to explore his options. Meanwhile, he began a systematic survey of his own experience to see what kinds of things he really liked to do. For a while, this produced a new source of conflict. Although he suspected that a life of thoughtful inactivity by some modern-day Walden Pond would answer his needs, she was equally sure that she could never be happy living in some isolated place away from her friends. ("I had my Walden," she said, "alone at home when the children were little.")

That storm passed, though, and they both kept working to find just what they really wanted, separately and together. Although an answer was slow in taking shape, both of them felt a great sense of relief in having acknowledged that the old way was no longer viable and that they were in transition. Although their new situation was far from comfortable, it was reassuring to know that most of what they felt was the natural result of transition rather than a sign of personal malfunction or interpersonal breakdown.

Their new beginning, when it did emerge, seemed almost ridiculously easy in comparison to the great effort they had expended in trying to find it. One day Don bumped into an old school friend whose father, a small-town newspaper editor in another part of the state, had just died. The friend had to sell the newspaper as soon as possible and he asked Don, who was the adviser to the school newspaper, whether he by any chance knew anyone who was looking for a small but successful weekly.

Before deciding to buy the paper, Don and Betty checked out the town with an eye to Betty's career. "If I'd gone along just for Don's sake, we'd have been back in our old pattern again," Betty said. "But it turned out fine. I got a job with the county mental health agency, and it's the perfect place to get the supervision I need to earn my license. We have a different kind of relationship now, although the transition was fairly rocky for a while. But both of us are happy, and we're learning new things about ourselves and each other every day. If we'd started over again with new partners, I suspect our new marriages would have ended up being a replay of our old one. But as it is, we're out on the frontier of our lives, exploring new territory."

TRANSITION, RELATIONSHIPS, AND RESONANCE

Transition would be a lot easier if the only issues a couple faced came purely from their current life situation itself—for Don and Betty, from their relationship and their conflicting needs for their individual satisfaction. But a situation like theirs is further complicated, as transitions often are, by the phenomenon of "interpersonal resonance," or the way in which the developmental issues being dealt with by one member of a family (or any group, for that matter) re-awaken or intensify similar issues in another. One person "resonates" to the situation or actions of another in the same way that one string on a musical instrument can be set vibrating when a nearby string is struck.

Don and Betty were the parents of two teenagers, and each of the children was in the midst of that extended transition toward personal independence that before long would (with luck) have them both standing "on their own two feet." At fifteen and sixteen, they were volatile: full of enthusiasm one day and ready to chuck everything the next. Bob exhausted new careers daily. First he wanted to be a test pilot, then an atomic physicist, then a computer engineer, and on and on. Meanwhile, he was slow to mature socially and didn't date at all.

Don found his son easy to understand yet strangely frustrating. Bob reminded his father of himself at fifteen—a crazy mixture of confidence and self-doubt—and Don sympathized with his son's confusions about himself. Not coincidentally, Don found himself very invested in Bob's career dreams. "I see him, so bright and capable in science and so interested in things I never dreamed of at his age, and I think, 'Go for it, kid! Don't take the safe route and be sorry later—the way I did.'"

At first Don explained his reactions to his son as "normal parental concern" for the boy's future welfare, but in time he began to wonder whether something more might be involved. "Here I am, stalled and lost at this transition point in my own life, and I can hardly stand to watch my son as he teeters back and forth on the edge of a big step in *his* life. When he finally applied to Cal Tech, I felt a sense of relief. It was more than pride—although I felt that too, of course. It was as though Bob was finally going to make something of himself and in doing that, to make something of *me*, too. He was my proxy, sent out to the world to do the business that I hadn't been able to finish. When I realized that, I decided, 'Hey, this isn't good for either of us. He can't do it for me, and my investment in him that way will just be a burden to him.' So I backed off."

This resonance between a child and a parent is common when the two of them arrive at different transition points at the same time. Betty found something similar happening to her when her daughter was going off to college. "I think that you're more excited by my departure than I am," Susan remarked to her mother one day. "It feels like you're trying to get rid of me."

In explaining that she did not feel that way, Betty discovered that the charge behind her reaction came from the same kind of proxy granting that Don had found himself doing with Bob. "She's heading out on her own," Betty said, in describing this discovery, "and her freedom stirs something very deep in me because I never gave myself that freedom. I don't think that I want it now, but I have to say that it really excites me."

Susan's freedom at this time included exploring her sexuality in several brief relationships. This alternately disturbed and amazed her mother. "Wouldn't you know that she'd be doing that just at the same time I'm reevaluating my marriage—when I'm still attractive to men and Don's turned off sexually!" It would have been easy, Betty realized, to transfer her own longings to her daughter. "I could stay faithful and live out my desires vicariously," she said with a little laugh. "But I guess it'll be better if I do my own business and let her do hers."

TRANSITION AND THE INTERPERSONAL SYSTEM

Families, like organizations and interpersonal groupings of all kinds, are "systems." That is, the members are not wholly autonomous entities that just happen to be together; rather, they are parts of a larger whole and are affected by anything that happens to that whole. It is characteristic of all systems that although their members may consciously try to change the way they behave within the system, they also often unwittingly perpetuate the system in its current form by undermining their own attempts to change it. Or they say they support a change that someone else in the system is trying to make, but under the table they try to sabotage the change.

A case in point. Don and Betty wanted their kids to launch out into the world, and each parent had a special reason to wish for that outcome—Don because of his own thwarted career dreams, and Betty because their independence resonated with her longing for freedom. Yet both of them also were scared of the transitions their kids were facing. "As long as they're at home, we're a *family*, and Don and I have something important to do together, which is to parent the kids." Betty certainly didn't want to stand in the way of her kids, but at this time of transition in her marriage she felt vulnerable. "If we aren't parents, what are we?" she asked Don on one occasion.

Many parents are far less aware than they were of this kind of resistance to change. "He's still a little boy to us," they say innocently of their thirty-year-old lawyer son. "She's not good enough for you," they say of the "girl" (who is, after all, thirty herself) that he is going out with. "Blood is thicker than water, son" (meaning that "nothing will ever replace your ties to us").

These reactions are not limited to parents whose children are leaving the nest or taking steps that will ultimately create a life structure of their own. Whenever a member of a system changes, the other members will feel a twinge. Children are bothered when divorced or widowed parents begin to date again. Siblings conspire to keep one another in line long after they have stopped living under the same roof. And, of course, partners in an intimate relationship react with alarm to unexpected changes in the other person.

Nothing makes it clearer how a relationship is structured with complementary roles than this reaction to the other person's transition. A husband may believe that he feels only supportive or even pleased when an important new beginning enters his wife's life, but then later he discovers that he is undermining it unwittingly. ("Really, I'm *thrilled* that you are going back to school—I don't know why I forgot my promise to cook dinner . . . pick up the kids . . . straighten the house before you came home.") It is as though the wife were in violation of an unspoken rule by being in transition.

Well, she is. Relationships are always structured by unspoken agreements, although people are seldom conscious of it. Beginning very early there is a psychological division of labor within a relationship: One person takes care of the practical issues and the other handles the human ones; or one expresses emotions and the other anchors the relationship in practical ways; or one is full of plans and the other is the tough critic. Each of them has always been somewhat that way—roles aren't invented out of thin air, after all—but the partnership lets them become more so. After a few years of that, the two are polarized with the role-enabled side of each personality artificially amplified by the arrangement. Each of them becomes a less-than-whole person, and each becomes a stand in for the side of the other's personality that is not being expressed within the relationship. He's not just a rational guy. He becomes the substitute for her rationality.

But then he discovers that life involves more than bookkeeping and contracts. Panic! The Rock of Gibraltar is crumbling! The other one's world begins to come apart when Old-Cool-and-Steady's transition leaves one flank exposed. The same thing happens if Sensitive-and-Warm begins to have ideas of her own about where she's heading and how to get there. Panic! The light of life is going out. The other one's world sputters and slows down, threatening to get stuck in some lonely byway.

This panic over a partner's change is natural. It's like the anxiety that an actor would feel if his cue produced no entrance and no response. Or worse yet, a response that isn't in the script. ("My God! She said *no*. She was supposed to say *yes*. How do I reply, and where does our drama go from here?")

Why is this? Are we so reactionary as creatures that we do not change unless someone else forces us to? Are we like pool balls, sitting forever in a fixed pattern until an interpersonal cue ball blasts us into motion? I think not, although we do suffer a kind of inner inertia when circumstances precipitate a transition. But it is not as mechanical as the table full of pool balls. Rather, we are more like stories that are slowly unfolding according to our own preestablished inner themes and plots. Each person's life is a story that is telling itself in the living of it, and each requires others to play certain kinds of roles. *(Wanted: A warm, unassertive woman to soothe a middle-aged and rapidly tiring knight on a decrepit horse.*) Each of us resists transition because a story is a self-coherent world with its own kind of immune system, and alien characters are out of place. (Think of trying to fit Dick Tracy into *Hamlet,* or Lady Chatterly into *Little House on the Prairie.*)

To become a couple is to agree implicitly to play a pre-arranged part in another person's story, although it sometimes takes a while to get the part down really well. It isn't enough to follow the overt signals, for the part might be that of the person who "never does what I ask you to do." An outsider listening to the dialogue would probably misunderstand the agreement between the two people. "He's urging you to go out and get a job," the outsider may say. "Why don't you do it?" But the person knows deep down that it is not so simple—that what the other one is really saying is something like, "You poor timid soul. You can't really face the world, can you? But that's all right because I'll take care of you."

This is all hidden from view, of course; or it is until one day the person—a wife in the traditional marriage—comes home and says, her heart in her throat, "Guess what. I got a job." And he says, "You *did?*" And he looks at her strangely, or says, rather unconvincingly, "That's wonderful." In a few minutes, he'll say, "Well, who the hell is going to pick up the stuff at the cleaners, then?"

A couple can find lots of help on how they ought to be: less sexist, say, or more open in their communication, or more accepting of each other. But they will have a far harder time finding help with the issue of how to change or how to let each other change within a relationship. This is unfortunate because in such a situation not only the relationship is at stake but also the ongoing growth of each partner individually.

In the next section of this book, we'll suggest strategies for dealing constructively with the transitions in our individual lives, but here we are talking about the developmental potentials of a relationship that is in transition. Whatever the current antagonisms and topics that a couple is trying to deal with, a life transition brings them to the point where each party has the opportunity to discover new inner resources that have hitherto been lived out mainly through the other person. Each of them has the opportunity to come out of the transition as a more whole, more complete person. Their relationship can then be renegotiated on a less restrictive basis.

This process of renegotiation must take place many times during a long-term relationship if it is to stay vital and provide both partners with the setting for their continued development. The process often happens unconsciously as each person deals with the other's transitions—and with the changing lives of any children they may have. It isn't necessarily a self-conscious procedure, like the arbitration of a labor dispute. It is simply the reorganization of the family system whenever an ending point is reached. And the process is greatly facilitated by the recognition that a relationship, like the lives that come together to form it, has its seasons and its times of turning. Problems, in that view, are not malfunctions to be solved or flaws to be corrected; they are the signals that a chapter in the joint story has ended.

When a couple can share this awareness and explore its significance in their present situation, they can transform even the most threatening difficulty into an opportunity. But if one of them cannot persuade the other to share this view and to join in this exploration, there is usually little choice but to begin the exploration alone. Of course, the great temptation is to pour your energy into trying to make your partner see things differently. When the first edition of this book came out, I got calls and letters from husbands or wives who announced that their spouses were in mid-life crisis (or in some other transition) and needed a talking to. I was always told that the partners in question "will listen to you." And that they really "need help."

That may have been so, of course, but it simply won't work to provide help that is not wanted at that point. What does work is for the partner who is aware of the transition and its implications for a relationship to begin exploring alone the question of what is ending in a relationship and what to do about it. More often than not, it turns out that the ending is not some external situation but an attitude or an assumption or a self-image that both partners have held. And the husbands or wives who were sure that their partners needed help find that the need is within themselves, that once the inner change is made by them, the other person proves to be not nearly so blind or unwilling to talk. I have come to regard it as more than likely that husbands or wives seeking help and advice for a spouse had better face their own need for help.

Some of the most difficult transitions within a relationship occur when the power center shifts from one side to the other. In a sense, this occurs the same way that other "separation of function" shifts happen. Many couples find that they have developed a tacit agreement that one member of the pair will make decisions for both of them. This arrangement is often rationalized by a comment such as, "He's so much better at finances than I am. I don't know a convertible bond from a small-cap stock . . . or whatever they're called." Or, "Her taste is a lot better than mine. Besides, I don't care so much about the whole living room *matching*—as long as the cushions are comfortable."

But these arrangements often change as the two people find the old allocation of rights and responsibilities are chafing them. "How come *you* always get to decide what we do on our vacations?" one of them demands one day. "How come we keep getting the car *you* want?" Pointing out that it's the way you've always done it doesn't cut much ice—as you may have noticed—and it is definitely a non-starter to run out a bunch of reasons that finally boil down to "I'm smarter than you are." Besides, the reasons aren't really the point, for these you-take-care-of-it-for-both-of-us arrangements generate a backlash. Most couples have been through several phases of such arrangements, first doing it one way and then the other.

One of the ways that you could divide the histories of most relationships into chapters would be by starting with "whose way we did things when we first got together," followed by "whose way we did things after that first arrangement broke down," followed by an alternating series of times when one or the other dominated the field of power. Sometimes, the shifts from one to the other are subtle and gradual; at other times, they are explosive: "That's it! I'm done with your something-or-other." But however they occur, the shifts are major transitions in the life of the relationship. Each time, both parties have to let go of how things used to be, go through a confusing neutral zone during which a new agreement is forged, and then launch the beginning of some new way of being together.

Throughout the transition, however, the parties will probably never articulate what they are doing or why. They may be "articulating" a lot of other things, though: what kind of a person one of them is, and what kind of a person the other is for putting up with that kind of a person. And so on. The argument is all about the content of the arrangement, but there is no acknowledgment of what is really going on. What *is* really going on? You might call it Rebalancing the Scales: taking things that have been skewed for some time back to "the other way for a while!" (though not "to the center," because that isn't the way power works within a system).

Not every issue affects the entire relationship, of course. The relationship is likely to be like a braid, one strand (providing financial support, say) going in the direction of one of the parties, another (deciding when to have sex, say) going in the other. Add to these "deciding whether to borrow money for a remodel," say, or "setting the time the kids have to be home," say, or "determining if and for how long relatives are welcome to visit us," say, and you have a whole weave of intersecting issues, the power patterns running first toward one side and then toward the other. When these patterns change, the parties to the relationship will report that they are in transition.

Various actions can help in that kind of a situation. First, of course, the partners should discuss what each of them is experiencing. Next, they should use the transition framework to structure that talk and to realize that relinquishing old arrangements and being left in the neutral zone is always difficult and confusing. The distress you feel isn't a sign that the other is being unfair, any more than it's a sign that you are defective. It's just that you are both in the midst of a significant life transition and it's taking its toll. Like any transition, this one could bring you out in a better place. You could well look back at it years hence and marvel at your inability to understand just what was going on. You could easily come to see it as the natural time of turmoil in between one chapter of your story and the next.

So hold all those possibilities in mind and use them as lenses through which to view your present situation in various ways. You may find that one lens clarifies things for one of you, but offers the other a distorted view. When you find that, recognize that the transitions are different for each of you and that they result in different views. It helps to imagine how it would feel if you had to relinquish the same things your partner is letting go. It helps to imagine the self-doubt that an anxiety producing new beginning may be causing the other. It helps to imagine how lost and confused the other feels when long-time patterns disappear and leave only a blank page to stare at in life's book.

Some specific things can assist you as well, and we'll close this chapter by listing several. Remember: No advice fits everyone, and no advice fits one person all the time. Just take what fits and leave the rest.

A checklist for people in a *relationship-in-transition*:

1. *Take your time.* The outer forms of our lives can change in an instant, but the inner reorientation that brings us back into a vital relation to people and activity takes time. This does not mean that everything must come to a standstill while you wait for things to work for you. But it does mean that your commitments, either to the old situation that you haven't yet left or to the new situation that you haven't yet become invested in, will be somewhat provisional. And it means that you cannot rush the inner process through which this state will change.

2. *Arrange temporary structures.* When I had my house remodeled a few years ago, for several weeks I tolerated a living room wall made of plastic and canvas. That temporary construction was ugly, but it provided me with the protection I needed to go on living in a space that was being transformed. So it is with transitional situations in the world of relation-

ships: You will need to work out ways of going on while the inner work is being done. This may involve working out a temporary way to make decisions; it may involve agreements about how to allocate responsibilities until something more permanent can be devised; or it may simply involve an inner resolve to accept a given situation as temporary and to transfer some energy to finding a replacement for it.

3. *Don't act for the sake of action.* The temporary situation is frustrating, so there is likely to be a temptation to "do something—anything." This reaction is understandable, but it usually leads to more difficulty. The transition process requires not only that we bring a chapter of our lives to conclusion but also that we discover whatever we need to learn for the next step.We need to stay in transition long enough to complete this important process, not to abort it through premature action.

4. *Take care of yourself in little ways.* This is probably not the time to be trying to live up to your highest self-image, although it is time to keep your agreements carefully. Be sensitive to your own small needs and don't force change upon yourself as though it were medicine. Find the small continuities that are important when everything else seems to be changing. A friend of mine took her elderly mother to the supermarket the day after she had moved to a new house and a new town. "Peaches, we've got to get peaches for your father," her mother said. It was the wrong time of year and peaches were expensive, but in a situation where everything else in their lives had changed, it was important to hold on to a few continuities such as favorite foods or a schedule of familiar TV programs.

5. *Explore the other side of the change.* Some changes are chosen and some are not, and each kind of transition has its own difficulties. If you have not chosen your change, there are a dozen reasons to refuse to see its possible benefits—for by seeing such benefits you may undercut your anger with the "adversary" who forced the change on you, or you may realize that the old situation wasn't all that you thought it was. On the other hand, if you have chosen your change, there are just as many reasons not to want to consider its cost—for that may weaken your resolve or make you aware of the pain your transition brings to others. Either way, you will need to explore the other side of the situation.

6. *Find someone to talk to.* Whether you choose a professional counselor or just a good friend, you will need someone to talk to when you are going through an important transition in your relationships. What you primarily need is not advice, although that may occasionally be useful, but rather the opportunity to put into words your dilemmas and your feelings so that you can fully understand what is going on. Beware of the listener who "knows exactly what you ought to do," but also be suspicious if you find yourself explaining away your listener's reactions whenever they don't happen to fit with yours—especially if several people have reacted the same way to what you say.

7. *Think of transition as a process of leaving the status quo, living for a while in a fertile "time-out," and then coming back with an answer.* The British historian Arnold Toynbee pointed out that societies gain access to new energies and new directions only after a "time of troubles" initiates a process of disintegration wherein the old order comes apart. He showed how often

the new orientation was made clear only after what he called a "withdrawal and return" on the part of individuals or creative minorities within the society. The needed transformation, it seems, takes place in an in-between state or outside the margin of ordinary life. That is so with individual lives as well: Things end, then you spend a time (or time-out) in the neutral zone, and then things begin anew. That is how life has always been and always will be. So make your time of transition a time of renewal and transformation. Come out of it stronger and better adapted to your world than you were when you went in.

4

Transitions in the Work Life

Whoever in middle age, attempts to realize the wishes and hopes of his early youth invariably deceives himself. Each ten years of a [person's] life has its own fortunes, its own hopes, its own desires.

—WOLFGANG VON GOETHE

TO GIVE PEOPLE'S LIFE STORIES ONE OVERARCHING shape, authors often trace their ultimate achievements back to a childhood dream. But that pattern is usually either the result of hindsight or a suggestion that their development was arrested by something early in their life journeys. As Goethe pointed out, the natural developmental pattern is not for people to keep the same dreams but to relinquish old dreams and generate new ones throughout their lifetimes. Most people also create new situations in the present, new hopes for the future, and new ways to realize those hopes. The image for such a life is not an upward-trending diagonal of increasing achievement but a spiral of linked cycles—the completion of each leading to a new cycle of experience and activity based on a new dream.

It is no wonder that a job, once a perfect fit with your talents and interests, ultimately becomes boring, or a career loses its power to take you where you want to go. Nor is it a surprise that in even the most rewarding and successful work life many people come to points where—often unexpectedly—they find themselves in transition. Sometimes the transition seems to rise up from inside—a wave of boredom directed at things they used to find interesting or a mistrust of things they used to believe in wholeheartedly; at other times, the transition is precipitated by external changes—either in their personal lives or in the organizations where they work. Either way, people usually try to put things back the way they used to be. If the transition is significant, however, that isn't likely to work.

In our culture, there are forces that stand in the way of this normal, cyclical pattern of development. We place a high value on monetary success and professional prestige, and that encourages people to set (and then keep trying to reach) distant and elevated goals. This emphasis on success often stands in the way of people's doing what really interests them and makes them happy. The elevated and distant goal of success is often rationalized by the idea that, even if the goal is not reached, its height insures that even falling short of it will lead to substantial achievement. For all but a very few, however, "aiming high" in that way guarantees an ultimate day of reckoning (and what a profound transition that is!) in which they will have to come to terms with having "failed."

"Aiming high" also means that the pay-off is so far away that your life may not provide you with the steady diet of meaning and gratification that comes from doing work that fits and expresses who you really are. And the emphasis on financial success not only dissuades people from careers and lives that they might have found very satisfying but also teaches them that their own imaginings and longings—those haunting feelings that they weren't meant to spend their lives doing what they're doing at the moment—are inherently untrustworthy guides. This sense (even though it is a misleading one) haunts them at each successive transition point, not only where they must once again establish a direction and tap into a renewed source of energy but also where they are bedeviled by the sense that they don't really know what they want or need.

This common impression—that your own changing ideas and dreams are not a reliable basis for planning your work life—leads many people to seek career assistance at life's natural transition points. People who have discounted or blocked out the inner callings from the future have cut themselves off from the very signals that really vital people use to stay on the paths of their own development. It is no wonder that people who have silenced those inner signals find meaningful careers difficult to launch and to maintain, or that when they encounter times of transition, they are so confused and distressed.

We will return to the question of the natural pattern of chapters that characterizes most vital and satisfying careers, but first we need to note that the extremely high level of change in today's organizations is likely to keep your career in a semipermanent state of transition. Reorganizations, mergers, technological changes, strategic shifts, and a steady stream of new products insure that most organizations are in a constant state of turmoil. Modern societies are the first in history in which people have been rewarded for keeping the level of societal change high. Most other times and places have rewarded and honored people for protecting the society's continuities; but our society rewards change in the name of "innovation." Our economy depends upon it, and if the innovation ceased, our economy as a whole—and, of course, most people's individual careers—would fall apart.

So we've got a change-dependent economy and a culture that celebrates creativity and innovation. There is no way that our ca-

reers *won't* be punctuated by frequent changes, each of which demands a transition from an old way of doing things and an old identity to a new one. And there is no way that these transitions *won't*
take a significant toll on our productivity as we temporarily siphon
off energy and time from performing our jobs to making the transitions. If that temporary displacement of energy happens to only a
few individuals, it is *their* problem; but when it occurs on a large
scale, as it does during big reorganizations and mergers, the individual problem of career transition[1] becomes *the organization's* problem, in the form of "reduced productivity," "absenteeism," "increased defects," or "turnover."

Whether at the individual or organization-wide level, transition
always reveals the same three phases that we keep returning to.
Whether the source of the transition is an external change or your
own inner development, the transition always starts with an ending.
To become something else, you have to stop being what you are
now; to start doing things a new way, you have to end the way you
are doing them now; and to develop a new attitude or outlook, you
have to let go of the old one you have now. Even though it sounds
backwards, endings always come first. The first task is to let go.

After that, you encounter the neutral zone—that apparently
empty in-between time when, under the surface of the organizational situation or invisibly inside you, the transformation is going
on. Everything feels as though it is up for grabs and you don't quite
know who you are or how you're supposed to behave, so this feels
like a meaningless time. But it is actually a very important time.
During your time in the neutral zone, you are receiving signals and
cues—if only you could decipher them!—as to what you need to
become for the next stage of your work life. And, unless you disrupt
it by trying to rush through the neutral zone quickly, you are slowly

being transformed into the person you need to be to move forward in your life.

How disruptive these times of reorientation will be during your career is determined by two things: first, the inherent importance of the change that triggers them; and, second, whether they coincide with a time when a developmental shift is occurring within you. Losing your job, for example, will always create a big change, but if it occurs when relatively little "developmental business" is going on inside you, it will simply be a practical problem that you have to solve. A much smaller change—not getting a promotion you had hoped for, for example—can have a larger impact on you if it occurs during a natural time of reappraisal and transition, like that at mid-life. A big change, for example, the death of your boss, will have a smaller impact on you when you are young and not so concerned with your own mortality than when you are in your sixties and dealing with the string of transitions that, together, comprise the process of "getting old."

Your own career transitions will also resonate with those that others are going through. When I was preparing to leave my teaching career thirty years ago, I had a sense (though I didn't yet know enough about transition to know why) that I needed some empty time between my old life and my new one. I was afraid that so long as I was still *a teacher* in my mind and heart, I'd be tempted to revert to that identity and style of being whenever I couldn't figure out what else to do. Although I was only beginning to understand life-transitions then, I had the intuitive sense that I ought to try to arrange things so that I could get by for some months with only short-term work while I was going through my transition. Fortunately, my wife was working almost full time and we had a little money saved up, so I was able to do that.

When I told members of my department about this plan, one of them said, "But where are you going to teach?" I explained that I wasn't going to teach anywhere for a while so that I could find a fresh perspective on my work life. My colleague looked dismayed, but said nothing. A week later, I bumped into him in the faculty dining room, where he was having lunch with another friend. "I was just telling Bob about your leaving the college," he said when I joined them, "but I couldn't remember where you said you were going to teach." When I reminded him that I wasn't going to teach anywhere, he denied having heard that before. "Not teach anywhere!" he said, surprised. "That's a big step."

I was confused by his reaction and wondered whether I had imagined our earlier conversation. Then a week later, he cleared up the confusion by "forgetting" again and being amazed for the third time by the news that I was really leaving teaching. He was unhappy with his own career, but had several years earlier decided that he was too old to make a shift. The workplace is full of such people—and they all have their own reasons for "resonating" to another individual's retirement, transfer, promotion, or firing.

A person's career, like the long-term relationships that we discussed in the last chapter, goes through a sequence of phases. To begin a new job is to encounter the same kinds of difficulties that one finds when beginning a new relationship. Each person undergoes a period of adjustment, although "adjustment" is a misleadingly mechanistic concept. It suggests that you need to fiddle with the dials and reset the switches to adapt yourself to the new situation. The trouble with this view is that although difficult changes must be made as one gets used to a new situation, the difficulty comes not from these changes but from the underlying and more difficult process of letting go of the person you used to be and then finding the new person you need to become in the new situation. The real difficulties, in short, come from the transition process.

It is important to understand how critical this transition process is to dealing successfully with work- and career-related changes. Being fired feels very different from changing a job intentionally, and both situations seem quite different from those mysterious doldrums that turn previously interesting jobs into purgatories. And all these seem different from taking a first job, or retiring, or being transferred. But under the surface of them all lies the experience of transition, and that experience brings about the distress rather than the problem of "adjusting" to the new situation. Not coincidentally, it is also transition rather than change that people notoriously resist.

Nor is it just the changes in the workplace that will affect your work life. Purely "personal" changes affect life at work, too. Even though you may think of your job and your family as worlds that are miles apart, whenever things are difficult at home, the energy and attention you bring to work are diminished. Your health, your finances, your sexual life, your spiritual world—none of those things can change without sending ripples across the world of your job and your career.

Sometimes, the change intensifies your energy, but more often it diverts energy from work to the area of your life that is changing. "I don't know what's happening to you," your boss may say in puzzlement. "You used to be such a hard worker, but lately . . . "

What's happening is, of course, the entire transition process; but someone who sees only the changes in motivation or results will probably try to reactivate the old motivation with encouragement, a change in job-assignment, or (failing with those things) by threats or punishments. These remedies miss the point, for you are not simply losing interest (which might indeed be re-stimulated) or growing tired of the same old stuff (in which case, a change might renew your interest). What is happening is that in ending and letting go of what you have been—which starts the transition process—you lose your old connections to the activities and the people that used to matter to you. In the turning cycle of change, this is the *fall*; attempts to reinstate your old motivations by reward or punishment are as futile as trying to keep leaves on the trees once they've started to fall.

To understand better what this means as well as what can be done about it, let's return to Don, the high school teacher in transition whom we discussed in the last chapter. None of his coworkers had a clear sense of what was going on in his life, but it was obvious to everyone that Don was doing a halfhearted job of teaching. When his principal talked to him about it, Don promised to try harder and left the conference feeling scared and confused.

Part of his confusion came from the gradual recognition that it wasn't just that home issues were undermining him at work; it was that *the same issues that were undermining him as a teacher were undermining him as a husband and as a father*. In all areas of his life, he felt a sense of emptiness and meaninglessness.

Don had unearthed a significant truth about his situation, and over the ensuing months he thought about it a great deal. In the process, he discovered one of the important transitions that is likely to take place in a person's work life sometime after the age of forty: the transition from being motivated by the chance to demonstrate *competence* to being motivated by the chance to find *personal meaning* in the work and its results. It is the shift from the question of *how* to the question of *why*.

The work world knows all about competence. Most evaluations and rewards are determined by a person's competence. Vocational guidance emphasizes it in testing which areas of work one would be most competent in. Transfers and promotions are based upon competence. In business and the professions, you get in and get ahead by demonstrating your competence.

But somewhere along the way—as early as thirty-five for some people, but as late as fifty-five for others—competence begins to lose its force as a source of motivation. The doctor says, "Yes, I'm a good surgeon, but the technical challenges just don't interest me the way they used to. What's the point of doing the same things over and over again?" And the plumber and the social worker and the housekeeper say the same thing. Of course, the old flame can be rekindled temporarily by shifting to an area where you must begin all over again and develop new competence, but the effects of such a change are usually short-lived. The season of competence is passing, in spite of some late-flowering transplants.

For months Don wrestled with the question of what he really wanted to be doing at this point in his life. But bit by bit, it became clear. Having spent most of his working life with ideas and theory, he longed to do something that involved practical action. He had always enjoyed working with young people, but now he longed for interaction with people his own age—people who wouldn't (he hoped) roll their eyes when he began ruminating about "what it all means." He liked writing, but he didn't have any books waiting to be born. And then he heard about the newspaper for sale.

It was a slow process, as most life transitions are. It meant working out ways of living with the transition process over many months. Don did it by holding on to his old job while he found what he wanted to do next. This was difficult because he was, as he said, "emotionally unplugged" from what he was doing. But having made sense out of that experience, he stopped fighting it. He found it tolerable and transferred his real energy to the larger undertaking of finding a new direction for himself.

Not everyone can make a vocational transition this way. If Don had been fired—which is always a possibility when you lose your interest in your work and stop working so hard at it—he would have had to find a way to support his family while he went through his transition. Perhaps the pressure to find a new career would have accelerated the transition process a little, although transition seems to have a timing of its own and a way of resisting efforts to rush it. If Don had been at some other point in his life, his transition would have involved different issues entirely.

Your work life, like your relational life, has its own natural rhythm. The task is to find the connection between the change in your work or career and the underlying developmental rhythm of your life. The books on adulthood offer some clues, but everyone's life history is unique. There is no litmus paper that will turn pink or blue in response to your life situation, and the task of finding the significance of a particular transition may be slow and difficult. Unless that significance is found, however, the thread of your personal development will be lost and you will be left with an inexplicable change and an overwhelming desire to put the pieces back together as quickly as possible.

Although there are no lists of Changes-and-Their-Meaning to tell you what a particular change means, there are ways of maximizing your chances of finding that meaning, and they apply equally to the world of relationships and the world of work. They start with two questions that you should learn to ask yourself whenever you are in transition. They'll help you to explore what the transition means in the developmental business of that particular time in your own life.

1. *What is it time to let go of in my own life right now?* This question marks the first difference between change and transition, for the latter must start with letting go. As we noted in "A Lifetime of Transitions," we periodically reach the point where an attitude, a belief, a style of responding to challenges, a goal or a dream for the future, or an assumption about others—that served us well up to that time—simply isn't what we need for the future. A young parent assumes that "there will always be time" to make up to children for the mistakes he or she has made—but then comes the day when the children have become *what they are,* and no major revisions are possible. Mid-life adults may still be making the provisional commitments that served them well in their twenties, when it made sense to keep lots of options open. But at fifty, that same kind of provisional commitment costs them the significant relationships and the big-league career opportunities that send you into the second half of life with momentum and meaning. Finding out *what* it is time to let go of often provides the way to initiate a transition meaningfully. Unfortunately, people are more likely to ask what new thing they can add to their lives. Even though they may get an interesting answer to that question, they won't be able to use it to make a meaningful transition because people have to start with endings—letting go of whatever it is time to let go of—before they can make new beginnings. If they fail, they find that even "great ideas" and "really exciting possibilities" simply do not help them. So start with *What is it time to let go of in my own life right now?*

2. *What is standing backstage, in the wings of my life, waiting to make its entrance?* The answer is something internal, some-

thing subjective, although it may be presented to you as an external event or situation that brings it to your attention. If it appears in its subjective form, it may take the shape of an idea or a fantasy or a question you ask yourself: "I've never worked for myself before"; or "Why didn't you ever follow up on that old idea of joining the Peace Corps?" It may present itself to you as an unexpected call from an old friend who wants to tell you about what he is doing these days, or as a fascinating story that you cut out of the paper that described a new social venture meant to divert young people from dangerous activities before it is too late. But whether it is a thought or idea you can't get out of your mind or an incident that interrupts the ordinary course of your life, this *thing* is like a message to you, a message that something is standing just outside the door of your everyday awareness, waiting for you to pay attention and invite it in. OK, so *what is standing backstage, in the wings of your life, waiting to make its entrance?*

I've called these the *first* and the *second* questions to ask yourself, because the letting-go process initiated by the first question—the process of making an ending—must clear the ground before the second process—let's call it "launching the next chapter in your life"—has room to develop. In reality, you will find yourself moving back and forth from one of these questions to the other. At one point, one of them may come into focus and feel like "the important thing right now"; at another point it will be the other that preoccupies you. Both of them are critical, however, and at any particular moment either of them may feel like the real issue.

As I noted earlier, everyone has a unique sequence of these endings and new beginnings, but there are also many similarities between these different lives. We've already mentioned some of them in our discussion of the riddle of the sphinx, which used that myth as a way to understand the three-phase pattern found in so many lives. Here we will do something similar with the Hindu idea about the four natural *seasons* of life, which will be the lens through which we view our work life transitions.

THE TIME OF APPRENTICESHIP

Sometime between their late teens and mid-twenties, most people cross an invisible line. Before they reach it, they are "getting ready to live life." After they've crossed it, they are living it—or would be, if they weren't so loathe to leave behind the sheltered waters of "getting ready." (As we shall see, it is common for people to be somewhat *retarded* in their development because of their difficulty with these big transitions at life's natural turning points.)

People often imagine that their sense of entering a new chapter of their lives at this time is the result of their having (choose whichever applies to you) taken a real job for the first time, left home to get married, or graduated from college. People who think that way are confusing cause and effect. They are changing inwardly, and the events of the external change serve to mark and symbolize the inward transition and the new stage of development that it makes possible.

Moving into your own apartment doesn't make you a separate, independent individual. But if you are growing into your own individuality right at that time, being out on your own feels huge! Being on your own at other times in your life may feel normal or sad or enjoyable or weird. But when the inner developmental business of your life is moving away from the dependencies of childhood into a world "of your own," then finding your own place to live is a big, meaningful step.

Work is a critical area in which this transition plays itself out. Whether or not you had a real "paying" job as a young person, your earnings back then weren't meant to support an adult life structure. And your identity was not something that you created through the work you did. More likely, you were still so-and-so's kid. And just as moving into an apartment of your own made you feel like a different person, so getting a job where you made enough to support yourself made you feel independent in a different way. That independence is all part of ending your reliance on parents.

Big transitions are happening at that time, and they are pieces of something even bigger: the end of life's first *season*, the time devoted to learning what's going to be expected of you by the world. As with all large transitions, the success of that time begins with letting go of the world that you were used to. As we have already said, traditional societies (and especially tribal ones) provided people with special rituals designed to amplify and dramatize the inner transition that was occurring then.

Not all societies stressed the *independence* of the person emerging from the stage of apprenticeship. Sometimes, the person simply assumed an adult role at that time; when that happened, the ceremony was thought of as a means of transforming one kind of person (a child) into another (an adult). The individual's new role (like the previous one) would have been largely prescribed; it was unlikely that the newly emerged adult could make choices about the person he or she wanted to be. Instead, the individual became the sort of person that his or her society expected and needed. But whether the turning point from life's first quarter to its second is framed (as in our world) as a time to make choices, or whether it is considered a time to leave behind the old childhood identity and take on the largely standardized responsibilities and privileges of adulthood, it is a major developmental turning point.

THE SHIFT TO HOUSEHOLDING

A young person who sets up a "household" at the end of the time of apprenticeship has taken a huge step forward. There are other steps, of course. Launching a long-term relationship with someone else—and, if the individual decides to, conceiving children with that person—helps to establish a young person as a full-scale adult. Instead of being part of someone else's world, these young people are building worlds of their own.

From the twenties through the fifties—and sometimes beyond—most modern people conduct the adult "business" of working and raising a family. In so doing, they are filling the role that the ancient Hindus called that of the *Householder*. This is a time of roles and responsibilities—a time when many modern people are not just "working" but pursuing a "career." In so doing, they develop expertise in their work as well as a greater understanding of it. If their work is conducted within an organization, they usually receive periodic promotions to higher levels of responsibility.

Two kinds of transitions characterize this long chapter in the lifetime. First, those that are triggered by the changes that happen to the organization for which the person works ("We've been acquired!" "The boss has been promoted and sent to London!" "The FTC has just ruled that our policy is illegal!"). Then there are changes to the individual: promotions and transfers, as well as less-tangible changes, such as the failure to get an expected promotion or the early retirement of a best friend at work. Each of those changes puts the person into transition, although organizations hardly acknowledge that state and expect people simply to *adjust* to the changes as they come along.

Early in a person's career, these changes and the transitions they trigger often carry echoes of the big developmental shift of getting out on one's own. A promotion, for example, may make you feel more solid in your independence, and the increased salary that it provides may give you the resources to express your individuality in some new way. The end of the *Apprentice* period may last for several years; meanwhile, you try, and reject, several different kinds of work, or sample several different settings in which you could do what you've decided to do. The transitions at work during that period will carry a developmental "cargo" that makes them feel bigger than they are.

Similarly, the transitions toward the end of your career are weighted down with the freight of what, in our society, we call "retirement." It is almost as though you were starting to "retire" a little at a time as the endings that initiate each of the late-career transitions in your work life cause you to let go of bits and pieces of the person you have been up to that point. Without formal transition machinery, such as the old rites of passage, we not only lack the support that traditional people enjoyed but also the powerful concentration that the old rituals provided—a power that took an extended and diffuse time of transformation and converted it into an *event*.

THE END OF HOUSEHOLDING

The modern work life lasts forty years, more or less. But somewhere around its mid-point, many people encounter a confusing time in which they are assailed by a sense—for some people vague and for others very intense and troubling—that "something has changed." This so-called mid-life transition occurs at the point in the lifetime when the Hindus believed that people were meant to stop being Householders and start the period of inner search and discovery that they called the *Forest-Dweller* phase.

The infamous signs of a mid-life crisis—the new cars, the unexpected divorces, and the sudden changes of behavior—are related to the transition that marks the beginning of this new phase, although they suggest that the person in transition is avoiding the real challenge of ending Householding and starting Forest-Dwelling. That challenges you to step back and reflect upon who you really are under the surface of the activities and the busyness of being a Householder. Making big changes at this point can easily be distractions from the real business at hand. They are often the signs that one is *avoiding* transition rather than embracing it.

Living out all the chapters of the developmental story would require at this point a review and reappraisal of the paths that you have been following through life. Failing to do that, they believed, would send you forward into the closing years of your career with the kind of unfinished business that will make its disruptive presence felt in the years ahead. The Hindus keyed the transition to Forest-Dwelling to the birth of one's first grandchild—the idea being that this was when the next generation took over the Householder function within the family.

In our time and place, of course, all this sounds strange. Far from stepping back to take stock, most Americans are engaged at that point in making the final assault on the mountaintop of success. But even though we don't acknowledge this natural transition point and incorporate it into our career plans does not mean that it does not exist. It does not mean that it is banished from our lives. It simply means that when we encounter it, we are unprepared.

In fact, the transitions that punctuate many people's careers after the age of forty or forty-five are the unmarked ruins of this natural time of transition. Whether such transitions take the form of a time when everything "goes dead," a time when things keep going wrong, a time when long-successful strategies suddenly stop working, or a time when the gray fog of depression covers whatever was once bright and interesting, this natural (if often delayed) time of transition starts with an ending, a sense of loss. And after we have acknowledged the ending, the sense of loss is replaced with emptiness, meaninglessness, a feeling that all our accomplishments actually mean very little. We say (if we have the courage to talk about the experience) that our careers aren't going anywhere; we may wonder whether we've been in the wrong career all along; we may consider an early retirement, although we probably at the time lack the funds to pull it off.

Those questions come from getting caught up in the content of our situation and from overlooking the underlying pattern. The feelings that we encounter at such a time are best understood as signs of a life passage that has been stripped of its rites and tossed aside as no longer useful. We are so distant from this sense that life has natural chapters, along with introductions marking transition, that we hardly know what we are missing. But life remembers . . . and tries to remind us.

THE FINAL CHAPTER

Now that the baby-boomers are passing mid-life, we are seeing an outflow of books about "modern patterns of aging" and "the new retirement." They all agree that this can be a rich time and that we need not stop working . . . if we don't want to. But they don't tell us much about what work naturally *means* during these years. They say that we may want to volunteer our time and energy rather than doing it for pay. They suggest that this is a time to find what we really want to do—the time of *have to* is past. They talk about recreation and travel and time spent with grandchildren. They offer advice on diet and travel and health, but they fail to help us create an appropriate final chapter to our work lives. "Retirement," at least as it has usually been defined, is not that chapter.

In the four-part Hindu scheme of life-long development that we have been drawing upon in this chapter, the final quarter of life is the time of the *Sannyasin*, the one who emerges from the Forest-Dweller phase of life with a much deeper understanding of life and the self than people have found in earlier phases. Just as the Householder phase represents the fruits of what was learned during the Apprentice phase, so the final chapter of the *Sannyasin* manifests and offers back to others what was learned during the Forest-Dweller phase.[2] What they have learned turns out to have a lot to do with transition because it involves the discovery that whatever you are now is the product of transition. Once your identity was nonexistent, and then it was new and untried. It was only through transition that you let go of whatever you then thought was critical to hold on to, and then you waited a while so that whatever was to come next could emerge and become the *new way* and the *new identity* that replaced the old.

You can learn that in the abstract earlier in life, but the only people who know it through living it over and over again are old people. Out there in The Forest, through taking stock of what life has taught them, the people who found a way to do the developmental business of mid-life discovered the deeper, the more spiritual meaning of transition. It is their own developmental task in the closing chapters of their lives to bring back that lesson to the world. It is their *business* during the final quarter of their life-long careers—what rubbish that careers end at any point before death!—to help people to understand the great alternating current of life, the rhythm whereby *being* is followed by letting go, which is followed by emptiness, which is followed by renewed energy and purpose, which is followed again by *being*.

The old need to grow into *wholeness*, to combine everything (negative as well as positive) into a ripened completeness, is what I described in *The Way of Transition* as the product of having been through transition often enough to understand the tremendous value of living through times when letting go is the only appropriate response to life. Important though perseverance is, old people know how easily it can turn into a refusal to get the message that life is trying to deliver. Being unwilling to accept defeat—though celebrated in the worlds of sports and warfare—is often a guarantee that one will never learn the lessons that must be learned if one is to mature. Elders need to help younger people learn that without releasing the fruits of one season, they cannot blossom into the next.[3]

The business of life's last quarter is to teach what was learned in The Forest. Elders are not supposed to inundate the young with truisms that too often pass for *wisdom*; they must show the young how to distill wisdom from their own experiences.

Our conventional idea of *retirement* does indeed need to be transformed, but all the talk about creative living arrangements for older people, rules permitting the elderly to keep their jobs, college study designed for lifelong learning, the foods and supplements that will "keep you young," and the investment vehicles that will assure a steady flow of income during the last quarter of life—all those things are diversions that distract older people from the work that needs to be done, both for society's sake and for their own. The final chapter of the work life may or may not involve salaried work, but it must return to society the fruits of those discoveries made during the third quarter of life.

I want to repeat here what I said back in Chapter 2: "The most important fact is not that there are one or three or four or six identifiable periods of crisis in a lifetime; rather, adulthood unfolds its promise in an alternating rhythm of expansion and contraction, change and stability." There is no list of stages that can represent this rhythmic pattern of growth. The stages vary from person to person; and even for a particular individual, it is difficult to put into logical terms just what a given phase of the work life is all about. I suspect that it is as much the process of exploring the question as it is an answer you may come up with that holds the benefit for you when your work life is in transition.

I will end this chapter by listing some questions that will help you explore the transition itself and its significance in the context of your life and career.[4] Consider setting aside an hour or two to reflect on them. You will probably find it helpful to write out your responses to the questions, both to capture the results of your thinking and because putting thoughts into words forces you to slow down and to articulate more completely what is in your mind.

1. What are the indications that your work life is in transition? Remember that a *change* in your work life is just that—a *change*—and that being in transition means that something more than that is going on inwardly. It means that you have

reached the point where it is time to let go of an idea or an assumption, a self-image or a dream. It means that you are moving from one chapter of your story to the next. Although that might involve being in between jobs, that is not the same as being in transition. A transition concludes when something new emerges from your own inner *neutral zone*, something around which you can build your new life. What emerges is not a new job—which would be a change—but some new sense of yourself, some new reality you're dealing with, some new idea that is moving you forward. Describe as well as you can what this current transition is—what it feels like, what it is doing to you, what it makes you think or wonder, and what it reminds you of. If the idea appeals to you, try *drawing* your transition, either as an abstract design or as a representational picture.

2. What is the developmental context of this work life transition? If you had to put into words the personal and career issues that you are dealing with at this point in your life, what would they be? If you had to give a title to the chapter of your work life that is drawing to a close, what would it be? And how about a title for this transitional introduction you are in now—what could it be called? And then—although this is hard, I know—what is the title of *the next* chapter of your work life? Oh, I know that you don't know! If you did, you wouldn't be reading this book, would you? Sure . . . sure. But consider the possibility that *at some level you already know what you need to do next*. Not "need" in the sense of "it would be good for you," but "need" in the sense of what has to happen so that you can take the next step in your life. You probably think that you don't know what the next chapter of your

work life is called, but that may not be true. You may just have mis-filed the information when you received it. You put it in the file marked "A Dream I Recently Had," or "A Crazy Idea I Just Know Wouldn't Work . . . But That Fascinates Me," or "The Books I've Found Myself Reading Recently." In other words, the future is not delivered like the morning paper; the future comes looking like something else. Don't be fooled. I think that even though you may not have told yourself yet in so many words, you know some very important things about the next chapter of your work life. Tell yourself whatever you know now.

3. Imagine that you are really old. Let's say you're ninety. From that time in the future, you can look back on yourself now. Then you'll know what was really going on now and even how things turned out. You may also know how they might have turned out if you had taken a different path. From that vantage point, was this present point in your life a time when it was a good idea to keep on in the same direction, or was it a time that cried out for change? And if the latter, what kind of change was called for? Looking back from age ninety, did you notice signs that pointed to the direction you ought to have taken at this point in your life, signs that may have been hard to see but that were there? And looking back from that future, what feelings do you have about your situation now? At ninety, are you sympathetic with your current confusion or impatient with your current blindness? At ninety, are you pleased by how things turned out or troubled by the nagging feeling that you missed a turn in the road back here where you're standing now? Do you, at ninety, wish you could have encouraged your present self to take more risks? Or do you

wish you could have made the present you wake up and see all that you already possessed and not risk it for something that was just ego candy? To give these questions a little more vitality, take a few moments first to imagine the old you that you'll be at ninety. Shut your eyes and see whether you can picture your ninety-year-old hands. Imagine what your old body will feel like in whatever position you are now in. In your mind, "people" the world that the old you will be living in: Who will be there, and who won't? Where will you be living? How will you spend your days? When you have let your imagination sketch out that world, try going back to any of the earlier questions that didn't seem answerable at the time, and let the ninety-year-old person who lives in that world answer the question.

And remember, you know more than you think you know!

PART II

THE TRANSITION
PROCESS ITSELF

Initiation is so closely linked to the mode of being of human existence that a considerable number of modern man's acts and gestures continue to repeat initiatory scenarios. Very often the "struggle for life," the "ordeals" and the "difficulties" that stand in the way of a vocation or a career in some sort reiterate the ordeals of initiation.

—MIRCEA ELIADE
The Sacred and the Profane[1]

HIS FACE AND BODY ARE WHITENED WITH CLAY, and he is no longer recognizable as the youth who left his village two months before. The wounds of his ordeal—a circumcision and the parallel scars across his cheeks—are healed now. But they will always bear witness to what he has suffered. They mark him as one who has crossed the boundary of childhood and has put that life behind him.

He is alone. More than simply out of contact with his peers and his elders, he is absolutely and radically alone. During this time (or time-out) in his life, he is out of relation with all others. There is no map to which one could point and say, "There he is." There is no *there*, because he inhabits for this time a nonplace.

He is beyond the mediating power of roles and relationships and social mores. Armed only with the rituals and chants taught him by an initiation master, he wanders free and unattached through the universe. Beyond the meaning-making powers of his everyday realities, he stands face-to-face with existence.

At night he dreams. His dreams in this primal nontime and nonplace are full of enigmatic hints and presences. Each night he goes to sleep praying that this will be the night of the great vision. It will be then and thus that he discovers his spirit guide or his guardian elder. That voice will tell him his true vocation and his real name. It may teach him a sacred chant to heal the sick or to bless the newly planted corn.

When this has happened, he will know the time has come to return to the village and take up the rights and responsibilities of his new status and his new identity. Marked by his scars and empowered by his new knowledge, he will rejoin the social order on a new basis. He is in a profound sense a new person.

The person he used to be is dead. It died in the ordeal and the mortuary ritual with which his rite of passage began. His parents signified his death by burning the sleeping mat he had used throughout his childhood. When he returns to the village, he will not recognize them—a least at first. For he is no longer theirs.

In the first weeks of his new life back in the village, he will not remember his old name. He is reborn, and for a time his behavior will recall that of a very small child. He will have forgotten how to do basic things—washing and feeding himself, for example. He will be unable to remember the old terms for familiar objects, although during his time with the initiation master he has acquired strange new names for many of these objects. To some degree, and on some occasions, he speaks a new language.

The youth has been renewed and enlightened by his ritual transition. The time-out in the nonplace was his gateway to the original chaos from which the gods fashioned the world in the beginning. All new form, his people believed, must begin in that chaos, and any gap in time or space may provide access to it. Such gaps occur at the end of any cycle. At the end of a year or a season, at the end of the reign of a chief, and at the end of a phase in the individual's own life, nature or the society or the person enters the gap and dies. After a time, each is reborn, and that is the way in which life sustains itself. It is the way of withdrawal and return. It is the way of forgetting and of rediscovery. It is the way of ending and of beginning. In following it, the person crosses over from an old way of being to a new way of being and is renewed.

This description of a youth in the middle of a rite of passage is a composite.[2] In one tribe, a tooth would have been knocked out, but there would have been no scars. In another place, it would have been a group of initiates rather than an individual that would have been isolated in the wilderness beyond the known village world. In some cultures, the initiation master would have been replaced by a circle of elders. In some groups, those elders would have planted the seeds of new understanding in the fertile ground of the gap; in others, they would have left the discovery up to the initiate's own vision and intuitions. The details of the ritual would have varied greatly from place to place, but the process of passage would have remained the same.

About a century ago, Arnold van Gennep, a Dutch anthropologist, first interpreted these rites for a modern Western audience. It was he who coined the term *rites of passage*, and it was he who pointed out that such rites were the way in which traditional societies structured life transitions.[3] He grouped together rituals dealing with birth and death, puberty and marriage; with the election of a chief and the creation of a shaman; with an individual's entry into a secret society of men or women and with nature's passage into a new season. He also saw that these ceremonial occasions consisted of three phases, which he called *separation, transition,* and *incorporation.*

During the first phase, the person or the group was separated from the old and familiar social context and put through a symbolic death experience. Then came a time in isolation in what van Gennep called the "neutral zone," a no-man's-land between the old way of being and the new. Finally, when the intended inner changes had taken place, the person or group was brought back and reintegrated into the social order on a new basis. Although some rituals emphasized one phase and minimized another, the passage rites all revealed this three-phase form to a remarkable extent.

Since van Gennep's time, a kind of nostalgia has built up around the notion of rites of passage. We moderns lack them, for the most part, and many people have remarked on this lack. Because we also have great difficulty with life transitions, some people think it logical that we could improve our situation by re-creating ritualized transitions. But rites do not transplant well. They are not techniques for doing something but lenses through which to magnify the experience of something. Rituals of passage are simply a way of focusing and making more visible the natural pattern of dying, chaos, and renewal that was believed to operate everywhere in the universe. And without that belief, there is nothing to focus. Unless a culture and its members see life transitions in that way, the rituals will be rejected like a transplant from an alien organism.

In its simple form, then, the nostalgia for rites of passage is misplaced. But the rituals are nonetheless important to understand. Developed in cultures that were less distracted than is ours by external changes and that were sensitive to the dynamics of personal transformation, passage rituals are our best records of the natural shape of personal change. Although they lacked our fascination with innovation and progress, these cultures were remarkably sophisticated in their understanding of the inner process of transition. Behind the strangeness of their surfaces, their rituals can provide us with the names for the elements of our own experience that are distressing and perplexing because they are otherwise nameless.

From here on, we will follow the lead of these cultures by examining the three natural phases of transition. Named "Endings," "The Neutral Zone," and "The New Beginning," these three component processes of personal change will be explored in detail so that you can understand why your own experience of transition takes the shape that it does, and how you can deal more constructively with it. For as the ancients knew, transition is the way to personal development.

Endings

What we call the beginning is often the end
And to make an end is to make a beginning.
The end is where we start from.

—T. S. ELIOT
"Little Gidding," from Four Quartets[1]

CONSIDERING THAT WE HAVE TO DEAL WITH ENDINGS all our lives, most of us handle them poorly. This is in part because we misunderstand them and take them either too seriously or not seriously enough. We take them too seriously by confusing them with finality—that's it, all over, never more, finished! We see them as something without sequel, forgetting that they are the first phase of the transition process and a precondition of self-renewal. At the same time, we fail to take them seriously enough. Because they scare us, we try to avoid them.

"I don't want to talk about the past," says a newly married man who has come in to talk about his second marriage. "I'm interested in the present and the future." How can I make him understand that his so-called present is a past that he hasn't yet let go of? His wife tried to tell him that when she yelled that he was still emotionally tied to his first wife. "No, I'm interested in us," he said. "It just bothers me when you do things the way she did. I want things to be different." But he doesn't want to talk about the past.

I try telling him a story: "Once there were two monks who were traveling through the countryside during the rainy season. Rounding a bend in the path, they found a muddy stream blocking their way. Beside it stood a lovely woman dressed in flowing robes. 'Here,' said one of the monks to the woman. 'Let me carry you across the water.' And he picked her up and carried her across. After setting her down on the far bank, he walked in silence with his fellow monk to the abbey on the hill. Later that evening, the other monk said suddenly, 'I think you made an error when you picked up that woman on our journey today. You know we are not supposed to have anything to do with women, and you held one close to you! You should not have done that.' 'How strange,' remarked the other. 'I carried her only across the water. You are carrying her still.'"[2]

I look at the man to see whether he has understood, but he hasn't. He wants to talk about his new marriage and finds my questions about his old marriage irritating. He wants to get on with beginnings. The hell with endings!

We all know how the man feels, and yet endings must be dealt with if we are to move on to whatever comes next in our lives. The new growth cannot take root on ground still covered with the old habits, attitudes, and outlooks because endings are the clearing process. No longer ritualized and formally prepared for us, endings happen to us in unforeseeable ways that often seem devoid of meaning—much less a positive meaning. Instead, they are simply events that we try to move beyond as quickly as possible. Even our language reflects this attitude: "Don't cry over spilt milk." "What's done is done." "Let bygones be bygones."

These attitudes were epitomized in that first transition class by the woman with the new baby who, objecting to our attention to endings, cracked, "I'm just trying to get used to having him, not sending him off to college." And her classmate who was getting used to the big promotion likewise found our concern for endings strange at first: "About all that I am giving up is low pay and low status," he said skeptically. But as we talked further, each of them discovered that the ending was not only real but important to understand and appreciate. For it wasn't the new beginning that accounted for the confusions they were experiencing but rather the termination of their old lives.

One of the advantages of being familiar with passage rituals is that they make it clear that the ending involves a symbolic death. When the new mother in the seminar shouted, "I am falling apart!" she was telling the truth—the "she" that she had hitherto identified with was disintegrating. Because of her view that disintegration meant malfunction, she assumed that what she needed was a way to repair her life; but she quickly came to see that no mere fixing up of things would suffice. All that good advice she kept asking for was beside the point, for her real need then was to find out how to let the person-that-she-had-been die and go through a renewal process.

The old passage rituals are one answer, though they depended on a social reality and a mythic imagination that is rare today. All the same, they provide a way of understanding the natural ending process and provide suggestive parallels to our own unritualized experience. To show how this is so, I will discuss the five aspects of the natural ending experience: disengagement, dismantling, disidentification, disenchantment, and disorientation.

DISENGAGEMENT

It seems to be a universal belief among traditional peoples that at times of inner transition people need to be separated from their familiar places in the social order. The young initiate is removed from the family, sometimes forcibly, and taken into the forest or the desert. The prospective shaman leaves the village and makes a long trek of self-discovery. The same thing happens at marriage and other transition points: entering a secret society, for example, or joining the circle of elders; or, finally, looking at death itself.

In stories of the ancient world, this step of disengagement is a common theme. Christ makes a forty-day journey into the wilderness; Theseus leaves the familiar world of Troetzen for the tests and ordeals of the overland journey to Athens. Sometimes in these stories the disengagement is undertaken unwittingly or with some other conscious intent, as though the everyday mind were unable to grasp the person's real need at such a time and so the person had to act *as if* he or she were not seeking disengagement. Jonah flees his vocation and heads to sea, but he believes that he is going to Tarshish. Oedipus leaves home to avoid a fate that, as it turns out, he meets along the way. Jonah and Oedipus both find that the first step toward destiny is taken in what they believe to be the opposite direction. And both find that, whatever the circumstances, there is a natural tendency to break with the familiar social matrix at times of life transition.

We no longer have oracles and visions—at least, we usually assume that we do not. No initiation master rings the bell one morning and says, "Your time has come." But all the same, we do find ourselves periodically being disengaged either willingly or unwillingly from the activities, the relationships, the settings, and the roles that have been important to us. What if these often distressing losses were really symbolic events? What if they were signals that a time of personal transition was beginning?

To ask such questions when the loss is fresh is often a pointless exercise and may even be a cruel one. The person who has just been fired or lost a parent or had a heart attack is not in the frame of mind to listen to talk about symbolic events—and certainly not to hear that it may be "a gift in disguise." But such people often come to such conclusions at a later point in the experience. Connie was a case in point.

She had originally approached me after a lecture to say that her husband was showing all the signs of a mid-life crisis, what-ever that was, and she wished that I would talk to him. He hadn't come to the lecture himself because he didn't think anything was wrong with him. "Hell no," he'd told her the night before. "I'm just catching on to what life is about, and I'm damned if I'm going to spend the rest of my life cutting along the dotted line!" In the few minutes that we talked, I gave her my usual explanation of why it seldom does much good to try to help someone who doesn't want help—and I suggested that perhaps she might be able to use some help on the question of where *she* was in her life just now. She looked dismayed. Clearly, I wasn't going to be of much help to her.

I ran into her three or four months later, and everything had fallen apart. Her husband had suddenly left one evening and was now living in a nearby city. During the following weeks, there had been some dreadful fights on the telephone, then some dreary ne-gotiations about money and about the children, and finally the start of divorce proceedings. "I can't pretend it's not all over now," Con-nie said sadly, "but I'd give anything if it weren't."

The main topics of our discussions at that point were practical—how to talk about the divorce to the kids, how to find work, how to deal with her parents, and how to start a social life again. Whenever the talk turned to the meaning of the separation, she'd say angrily, "You'll have to ask him. He was the one who did it."

In time, however, this changed. She began to talk about what she had lost. She had lost a great deal of security, for one thing, because the family income all came from her husband's work. She had lost companionship, for although he had traveled a good deal, she had never felt "alone in the world," as she put it. She had lost a sexual partner, too, and a confidant—as well as a critic and an instructor. When I pressed her to explain these last losses further, she said sadly and softly, "My self-esteem, as a woman and as a person, was all tied up with his reactions to me. I didn't just lose a husband. I lost my way of evaluating myself. He was my mirror. Now I don't know how I look any more."

It is not underestimating the seriousness of her other losses to say that this was the biggest one. But neither is it underestimating the gravity of the loss of her mirror, as she called it, to say that it represented an opportunity for development. It was a long time before she would call it that, however, for the natural process of grieving is sometimes a very slow one. But within a few weeks, she was beginning to talk about a sense that she had come to a time in her life where she no longer needed to rely so much on others for an estimate of how she was doing. This view of things grew on her, and she brought it up more frequently, until one day she came in and announced that she had decided the divorce was no random accident in her life. "Any earlier and I wouldn't have been ready; any later and I'd have been so hopelessly invested in our system that I'd have died when it was broken. Yes, it came just at the right moment."

Connie's transition was a turning point in her life; it left her a stronger and more vital person than she had been before. It had begun with an ending, and the ending had begun with a disengagement. Connie had been deprived of the familiar ways of knowing herself by the separation from her husband, and this provided her with an opportunity that would have been hard to find within their relationship. (This is not to say that divorce was necessary—only that some significant disengagement was an important element in making her change.)

Divorces, deaths, job changes, moves, illnesses, and many lesser events disengage us from the contexts in which we have known ourselves. They break up the old cue system that served to reinforce our roles and to pattern our behavior. It isn't just that the disappearance of the old system forces us to devise a new one, the way that a breakdown in the economic order might lead to barter. It is rather that as long as a system is working, it is very difficult for a member of it to imagine an alternative way of life and an alternative identity. But with disengagement, an inexorable process of change begins. Clarified, channeled, and supported, that change can lead toward a development and renewal.

DISMANTLING

Getting unplugged from your old place in the interpersonal and social world that gave you an identity is where the transition process starts, but disengagement only stops the old signals and cues from being received. It leaves untouched the life infrastructure that you've constructed in response to those signals. The disengagement can take place in a moment: "I'm leaving! We're finished! Goodbye!" But the old habits and behaviors and practices that made you feel like yourself can only be "dismantled." They have to be taken apart a piece at a time.

We hear a lot, thanks partly to the important work done by Elizabeth Kubler-Ross, about the stages of the "grieving process," that string of emotional states starting with denial and ending with acceptance, through which people who are coming to terms with a loss typically go. But there is a parallel and separate process that we don't hear so much about that is not so much emotional as it is cognitive. It is the one in which people in transition gradually stop thinking of themselves as part of a *we* and start thinking of themselves as an *I*. Let's call this one the "mourning process." This shift is often accompanied or punctuated by a good deal of emotion, but those feelings are reactions to the process, not the process itself.

By not distinguishing between these two aspects of making an ending, many people imagine that a person who is wracked with emotion after a loss is doing important inner work; and that a person who is not, is not. They look at societies where grieving is formalized and highly stylized and imagine that these practices help people to get through or "over" the experience of loss. What such people usually overlook are the parallel prescriptions and practices that provide people with a set of practical stages to go through: For three days you keep a vigil over the lost one; on the thirtieth night after the death, you have a ceremony; you wear only black for a prescribed period, and you hold a remembrance ceremony on the anniversary of the death. And as you do these things, you slowly *dismantle* or *unpack* your relationship to the person, or the relationship or identity that you have lost.

One of the huge transitions that occurred in my own life between the original publication of *Transitions* and this revision was the death of my first wife from cancer. In *The Way of Transition*

(2000), I have described that experience and its effect on me in some detail, so I will not repeat that here—only say that the most unexpected part of my coming to terms with that loss was the long slow process of *dismantling* my old world and the identity I had built in it.

Ironically, I happened to be remodeling my home at that same time. I remember sitting in the living room, which was stripped down to bare studs and siding, electrical wiring criss-crossing over-head and breaks in the subflooring showing the outlines of the now-vanished floor plan underfoot—sitting there and thinking, what a perfect metaphor! Dismantling my house while I dismantle my life! Still able to see the signs of how it used to be, but watching as, day by day, those were covered over or replaced by new "construction."

Anyone who has ever remodeled a house knows a good deal about personal transition because such an undertaking replicates the three-part transition process: It starts by making an ending and de-stroying what used to be. Then there is the time when it isn't the old way any more, but not yet the new way, either. Some dismantling is still going on, but so is some new building. It is a very confusing time, and it is a good idea to have made temporary arrangements for dealing with this interim ("neutral zone") state of affairs—whether it is temporary housing or a time of modified activities and reduced expectations to make the old housing work. And as the contractors always warn you, remodeling always takes more time and money than new construction. Good advice in regard to transition, too.

DISIDENTIFICATION

In breaking your old connections to the world and taking apart the internal structures required by those connections, you also lose your old ways of defining yourself. Connie's way of putting it was that in divorcing her husband she had "lost her mirror." Others feel it as the loss of a role that prescribed their behavior and made them readily identifiable; still others feel the lack of a familiar and identifying label. One way or another, most people in transition have the experience of no longer being quite sure who they are. This experience corresponds to an important element in most passage ceremonies: the removal of the old identity's signs and the temporary assumption of a nonidentity, which is represented by shaved heads, painted faces, masks, strange clothing or no clothing at all, or the abandonment of one's old name.

This disidentification process is usually the inner side of the disengagement process. It is often particularly distressing in vocational transitions, or where the old roles and titles were an important part of the person's identity. The impact of such losses can be much greater than one imagines it will be.

I had thought about this loss a good deal when I was leaving my teaching career, for example, and I was convinced that I had thought it through and had come to terms with "not being a teacher any more." Then one day my youngest daughter came home from school and asked casually, "What are you, Daddy?" I began one of those long and careful replies that rapidly exhaust a child's interest in the subject being discussed. I told her how I used to be a teacher (the past comes in handy when the present isn't very clear) and how I was now partly a lecturer and partly a writer, and how I did some counseling and consulting. Then, seeing that I was losing her, I said, "Why do you ask?" "Oh, we're talking at school about what our daddies do, and I wondered what I should say."

This troubled me for weeks. I had thought that I was comfortable with my temporary state of disidentification, but I found that I was vulnerable through the kids—who didn't really care *what* I did, so long as it had a name. As time went on, I grew more comfortable with what might be called a "participial" identity, that is, identifying with *ing* words (gardening, writing, running, lecturing) rather than with nouns. But I have to admit that it always bothered me that the kids preferred nouns. They corresponded to the part of me that still longed for the lost security of a recognizable label. Teacher, college professor, the Aurelia Henry Reinhardt Professor of American Literature at Mills College. Ah, those were the old days! But now, gardening and running? ("Whatever happened to Bridges, anyhow?")

On the other hand, I sometimes found pleasure during that period in imagining that I was in the middle of a secret passage ritual. In a world of social identities, I was an interloper. I lived in the cracks and moved in the shadows. My own passage markings were hidden and secret, but I was being initiated into the next phase of my life—into middle age, for lack of a better term. I had shed the shell of my old identity like a lobster, and I was staying close to the rocks because I was still soft and vulnerable. I'd have a new and better-fitting identity in time, but for now I'd have to go a little slowly.

I found it useful then to reflect more seriously on why being disidentified was an important part of the termination process. Clearly, the old identity stands in the way of transition—and of transformation and self-renewal. I could appreciate the wry wisdom in the sign that Erik Erikson reports having seen over a bar in a Western town: "I ain't what I ought to be," it read, "and I ain't what I'm going to be. But I ain't what I was!"

At other times, though, disidentification is no laughing matter. No longer being *Bob's wife* or *a salesman*, no longer being the *old me* or *a young person* is a source of panic. That is when it is important to remember the significance of disidentification and the need to loosen the bonds of the person we think we are so that we can go through a transition toward a new identity.

DISENCHANTMENT

Separated from the old identity and the old situation or some important aspect of it, a person floats free in a kind of limbo between two worlds. But there is still the reality in that person's head—a picture of the "way things are," which ties the person to the old world with subtle strands of assumption and expectation. The sun will rise tomorrow, my mother loves me, the tribe will endure, the gods are just: These things are *so*, and if they are not, then my world is no longer real. The discovery that in some sense one's world is indeed no longer real is what is meant by disenchantment.

In traditional rites of passage disenchantment was a carefully arranged experience.[3] In the ceremony for entry into the healing cult of the Ndembu of Africa, initiates were brought before a strange shape in the jungle; they were told this was Davula, or the cult's spirit. Then unexpectedly they were told to beat on the spirit-shape with sticks and kill it. At the end, they were shown that the thing they had beaten was nothing but a cloth-covered frame under which adepts had been hiding. A similar process took place in other passage ceremonies: when Hopi youths saw the awe-inspiring kachinas (who were actually neighbors and relatives) unmask for the first time, or when terrified initiates in aboriginal Australia were shown that the fearful sound of the great spirit Dhuramoolan was nothing more than a bull-roarer, or flat piece of wood on a thong.

This may remind you of the disenchantments of your own childhood: that there is no Santa Claus; that parents sometimes lie and are afraid and make stupid mistakes and like silly things; that best friends let you down. But these disenchantments did not end with childhood—nor are they over yet. The lifetime contains a long chain of disenchantments, many small and a few large: lovers who prove unfaithful, leaders who are corrupt, idols who turn out to be petty and dull, organizations that betray your trust. Worst of all, there are the times when you turned out to be what you said (and even believed) that you were not. Disenchantment, you can quickly discover, is a recurrent experience throughout the lifetime of anyone who has the courage and trust to believe in the first place.

Many significant transitions not only involve disenchantment, they begin with it. But like the other aspects of the termination process, it may be that the person can only slowly begin to see the disenchantment experience as meaningful. When you discover the fatal love letter or get the news that you've been fired, it's pointless to talk about old realities and new ones. But later, it is important to reflect on these things, for with realities as with identities and connections, the old must be cleared away before the new can grow. The mind is a vessel that must be emptied if new wine is to be put in.

This process is hard to take in more than just a natural, personal sense; it goes against the grain of our culture, which tends to view growth as an additive process. We did not have to *unlearn* the first grade to go on to the second, for example, or forget Sunday school when we joined the church. We do not expect to give up old beliefs (in spite of St. Paul's injunction to "put away childish things") in order to mature. In fact, the entire termination process violates our too-seldom examined idea that development means *gain* and has nothing to do with *loss*.

The Western mind has worked this way for a long time. Odysseus, you will remember, found it terribly difficult to let go of his assumptions about reality. The world was a battlefield that required armor and struggle. He had been a winner by those rules, and it made no sense to him suddenly to find them not working at Ismaros or in the narrows between Scylla and Charybdis. He found that the first task of transition was unlearning, not learning anew.

The lesson of disenchantment begins with the discovery that if you want to change—really to change, and not just to switch positions—you must realize that some significant part of your old reality was in your head, not out there. The flawless parent, the noble leader, the perfect wife, and the utterly trustworthy friend are an *inner* cast of characters looking for actors to play the parts. One person is on the lookout for someone older and wiser, and another is seeking an admiring follower. And when they find each other they fit like the interlocking pieces of a puzzle.

Or almost. Actually, the misfit is greater than either person knows, or even wants to know. The thing that keeps this misperception in place is an "enchantment," a spell cast by the past on the present. Most of the time, these enchantments work fairly well, but at life's turning points they break down. Almost inevitably we feel cheated at such times, as though someone were trying to trick us. But usually the earlier enchanted view was as "real" as we could manage at the time. It corresponded to a self-image and a situation, and it could not change without affecting ourselves and others.

The point is that disenchantment, whether it is a minor disappointment or a major shock, is the signal that things are moving into transition. At such times, we need to consider whether the old view or belief may not have been an enchantment cast on us in the past to keep us from seeing deeper into ourselves and others than we were then ready to. For the whole idea of disenchantment is that reality has many layers, none "wrong" but each appropriate to a particular phase of intellectual and spiritual development. The disenchantment experience is the signal that the time has come to look below the surface of what has been thought to be *so*. It is the sign that you are ready to see and understand *more* now.

Lacking that perspective on such experiences, however, we often miss the point and simply become "disillusioned." The disenchanted person recognizes the old view as sufficient in its time, but insufficient now: "I needed to believe that husbands [or friends or mentors] were always trustworthy; it protected me against some of the contingencies of life." On the other hand, the disillusioned person simply rejects the embodiment of the earlier view; she finds a new husband or he gets a new boss, but both leave unchanged the old enchanted view of relationships. The disenchanted person moves on, but the disillusioned person stops and goes through the play again with new actors. Such a person is on a perpetual quest for a *real* friend, a *true* mate, and a *trustworthy* leader. The quest only goes around in circles, and real movement and real development are arrested.

DISORIENTATION

The "reality" that is left behind in all endings is not just a picture on the wall. It is a sense of which way is up and which way is down; it is a sense of which way is forward and which way is back. It is, in short, a way of orienting oneself and of moving forward into the future. In the old passage rituals, the one in transition would often be taken into unfamiliar territory, beyond the bounds of former experience, and left there for a time. All the customary signs of location would be gone, and the only remaining source of orientation would be the heavens. In such a setting and the state of mind it was meant to create, you would be (in the words of Robert Frost) "lost enough to find yourself."

As with other aspects of the ending process, most of us already know disorientation. We recognize the lost, confused, don't-know-where-I-am feeling that deepens as we become disengaged, disidentified, and disenchanted. The old sense of life as "going somewhere" breaks down, and we feel like shipwrecked sailors on some existential atoll.

One of the first and most serious casualties of disorientation is likely to be our sense of (and plans for) the future. The guy who is fired (disengagement) or bypassed for promotion one last time (disenchantment) is likely to find himself losing interest in old goals and plans. This loss of motive power and direction is frightening to many individuals and those around them, and it may in fact be dangerous in a practical sense if it threatens the essential arrangements of a person's life.

It would be a mistake in such situations to view disorientation as positively as one can in retrospect. Traditional people in passage did not enjoy or embrace the experience of disorientation. They suffered through it because *that was the way*, which is to say because they had faith in the process of death and rebirth. Because they had that faith, they did not need to make distress comfortable. However, many modern people lacking that faith are caught between positive thinking and despair; they keep themselves going only by lighting matches and whistling in the dark.

There is a danger that what I am saying about disorientation and the ending process in general will become merely a rationalization or an anesthetic for personal distress: "Hey, isn't that wonderful! I just bumped into a tree. I must be *disoriented!*" To do that is to deny the real experience and to vitiate the transition. Disorientation is meaningful, but it isn't enjoyable. It is a time of confusion and emptiness when ordinary things assume an unreal quality. Things that used to be important don't seem to matter much now. We feel stuck, dead, lost in some great, dark nonworld. No wonder that many myths depict this state as one in which the hero is swallowed and trapped in the entrails of a great serpent or fish. No wonder that a hero's path at that point was the convoluted way through a labyrinth.

Disorientation affects not only our sense of space but also our sense of time. I talked with a man recently who had just stopped smoking. "Where did all the extra time come from?" he asked half seriously. "I must have used up hours and hours smoking." And that is so, to some extent. But the changed time sense also comes from the ending of a familiar way of structuring time. Several times an hour this man was used to taking out matches and cigarettes and going through a familiar set of actions. Although time lapses between cigarettes might have varied, he could have marked the passage of time by the butts in the ashtray. When he stopped smoking, time stretched before him like the open sea.

That often happens in transition, and some of our resistance to going into transition comes from our fear of this emptiness. The problem is not that we don't want to give up a job or a relationship, or that we can't let go of our identity or our reality. The problem is that before we can find a new something, we must deal with a time of nothingness. And that prospect awakens old fears and all the old fantasies about death and abandonment.

THE OEDIPUS COMPLEX—ANOTHER VIEW

The ancient story of Oedipus is full of wisdom concerning the way in which a phase of life comes to an end. We are most familiar with interpretations of the myth as an account of the effects of romantic rivalry in childhood—Freud having said that all men wish to destroy their fathers and marry their mothers. But Sophocles' *Oedipus Rex* seems to me to disclose more about life in general if it is viewed as a myth about transition. Because we need to set aside our preconceptions about this play if we are to see it afresh, I suggest that we view it not as a famous tragedy or as the basis for psychoanalytic theory but as it would be if it were your own dream. In viewing it that way, you can relate it more directly to the deeper levels of your own experience.

Imagine that you wake suddenly in the middle of the night and lie there, frightened and confused by a strange dream. In it, you are standing in a great square, surrounded by the façades of temples and palaces. Before you there is a large crowd of townspeople, some kneeling or standing, some lying down with illness and fatigue. All of them are looking at you with a mixture of desperate hope and fear in their eyes. They are silent except for an occasional child's whimper or a moan from one of the sick. Wordlessly, these people are beseeching you to save them from something.

Then a spokesman steps forth from the group and addresses you directly. Calling you *ruler*, he says that the city is under a curse. The crops are withering in the fields, and the herds are weak and dying. Women are bearing stillborn children, and sickness is everywhere.

Before you have time to reply, he reminds you how you came to be the ruler of this land. The city was at that time, too, in the grip of a curse, as the terrible sphinx crouched outside the city gate and refused to give back life to the city until someone answered the sphinx's riddle about the animal that walks on four feet in the morning, two at noon, and three in the evening. You were a young adult then, just beginning to make your own way in the world, and you stepped forth and risked an answer: *the human being*, you said. You solved the riddle, the spell was broken, and in gratitude the city made you its ruler.

So now the spokesman says, "Do it for us again." [In the play, he puts it more cunningly: "Never be it our memory of thy reign that we were first restored and afterward cast down by you."] They are asking you to keep on being the one you have always been—to live up to your public image. They ask you *not to change* now.

And that is where the dream ends, but long after you have risen, the dream stays with you, nagging at you and drawing your attention away from the practical business of waking life. What a compelling argument: Do it again . . . don't change now . . . live up to your image . . . keep on being *the old you*. The dream and its argument stir something deep in you. It blends with your daily activity in a strange way that becomes suggestive. Holding the dream shape in your mind, you think about what is going on with you just now. Dream and life correspond somehow, like a sketch and a face. And then you realize.

From home, from work, even from your own mind comes the appeal to continue being the one you've been. Don't change. Do the old, familiar thing again. Just when you feel drawn toward new beginnings, powerful inner and outer forces are blocking the way. The dream is your life.

The Oedipal situation, viewed in this context, is not the triangular pattern of mother, father, and child, but rather the situation of the adult who is torn between the developmental thrust that brings about life transitions and the impulse toward repetition that aborts them. Viewed symbolically, the withering crops and the stillborn creatures are the dying of an old life phase and the feelings of deadness that so often signal the start of the termination process.

The story of Oedipus is thus a symbolic representation of what goes on in our lives when we seek to hold on to an old and outlived way of being in the world. The old way is the source of the curse, as Oedipus finds when he sends for counsel from the oracle at Delphi. The oracle says that some "defiling thing" is the cause, and that the thing is the presence in the city of the former king's killer. Now, that murderer is Oedipus himself; for on his way to the city twenty years before, he had encountered a man at a narrow place in the road and argued with him over the right of way. The older man tried to run him down, and the young Oedipus fought back and killed him—not knowing that the man was King Laius, his own father.

But the killing itself wasn't the source of the trouble, for the gods brought Oedipus to the city, placed the right answer in his mouth, made him a hero, and let Thebes prosper for twenty years under his scepter. Viewed symbolically, that killing was the natural and necessary act of its time. Like many parents, this mythic father blocked his son's way and denied his right to emerge into his own. Becoming independent and finding his own place in the world entailed a symbolic slaying of the parent and the dependency that had once been necessary.

But Oedipus had long since finished with that developmental business of early adulthood. That phase of life (the *heroic* phase, in mythic terms) was done and something else was ready to take its place. This natural and inexorable succession of life phases was, as we noted in Chapter 2, the very point of the sphinx's riddle. Like many of us, Oedipus knew the "answer" but failed to apply it in his own crucial and complex life situation.

Oedipus is right at the second great transition point in life, the time when he must leave his involvement and identification with the social roles and self-images that have been successful. Now, however, there is no outer enemy. There is only the puzzle-solving, dragon-slaying man who sees the world in terms of outer enemies— a man trying to perpetuate an outlived way of being and acting. There is only himself, and he is behaving in a way that fitted its time but has now "polluted" a time that calls for something else.

So what does he do? He sends to Delphi for the answer. (The old puzzle solver will set things right!) And the answer is that the murderer of Laius is defiling the city. Oedipus announces that he will find the man and he will banish him. (The hero rides again!) He brings to bear on this time of life transition the very approach to things that life is calling upon him to give up. And in the process, the hero slays "the hero" in himself.

The story of Oedipus illuminates the process of life transition. It shows that after a certain point the very ways of being that brought forth and sustained a life phase begin to destroy it. This happens more than once in the play. Shortly after he was born, and long before the play began, Oedipus was sent away because of a prophecy that he would one day kill his father. Later, when he learned of the prophecy, he left his foster parents' house. At each step, the attempt to perpetuate something is the act that initiates its downfall. Our endings, we must discover, are often brought about by the very acts and words that we believed would keep things the way they have always been.

The myth suggests a morality that is deeper than any code of social ethics, and it comes from a natural order that moves to the rhythm of life itself. The goal of one phase of life becomes the burden of the next. That is why rites of passage begin with a symbolic death. Without that death, the life becomes "polluted," as the oracle said the city of Thebes had become.

Having so strenuously resisted the summons to change, Oedipus suffered terribly in the process of transformation. But we often overlook the sequel to *Oedipus Rex*. Sophocles meant us to see that after the death came a rebirth and a new way of being in the world. By the time we meet Oedipus again in *Oedipus At Colonus*, he has passed through the suffering of loss. Leaning on the cane that the sphinx's riddle had referred to, he is not just old but is spiritually enlightened and a blessing to whatever town harbors him.

Oedipus's story makes us realize that we are likely to resist and misunderstand significant transitional changes—at a time when it is terribly important to seek another perspective. Oedipus sent to Delphi for counsel, but he misread the oracle's reply. He called in the great seer Tiresias, but he refused to hear what the sage told him. He tried to fit the new information into his old reality, but in the end the disenchantment took place and he understood what had happened.

WHAT IT IS TIME TO LET GO OF

One of the most important differences between a change and a transition is that changes are driven to reach a goal, but transitions start with letting go of what no longer fits or is adequate to the life stage you are in. You need to figure out for yourself what exactly that no-longer-appropriate thing is. There's no list in the back of the book. But there is a hint that can save you considerable pain and remorse: Whatever it is, it is *internal*. Although it might be true that you emerge from a time of transition with the clear sense that it is time for you to end a relationship or leave a job, that simply represents the *change* that your *transition* has prepared you to make. The transition itself begins with letting go of something that you have believed or assumed, some way you've always been or seen yourself, some outlook on the world or attitude toward others.

Looking back at the five words starting with *dis*, note that only "disengagement" refers exclusively to external things. "Dismantling" can be either an internal or an external process, and "disidentification," "disenchantment," and "disorientation" all refer to internal things. It is the internal things that really hold us to the past, and people who try to deal only with externals are people who walk out of relationships, leave jobs, move across the country . . . but who don't end up significantly different from what and who they were before. They are likely to be people who have learned to use *change* to avoid *transition*. They storm out of a job ("rotten, no-good boss!") rather than discover what it is in themselves that keeps finding such bosses to work for. They end another (yet *another!*) relationship rather than let go of the behaviors, attitudes, assumptions, and images of self or others that keep making relationships turn out this way.

In making this important point, I don't want to leave the impression that endings never involve an external change. My point is simply that the inner ending is what initiates the transition. You see, change can lead to transition; but transition can also lead to change. People who move to another town and embrace a new way of life are making changes that will put them into transition; that is, change leads to transition. But they may have made that move because they are starting to seek different things from life, because their old habits don't fit them any more, because inwardly they've become new people; that is, transition leads to change.

Because of this situation, the "endings" that launch transition usually come either before or after the "endings" that are part of change. I was reminded of this recently when a friend was talking about the breakup of his marriage. "But, you know, it really ended quite a while before she left," he said. "In fact, it was over months before, but I wasn't ready to face that fact. It was only when she actually walked out that I could admit it was over."

As I listened to him, I thought back to the day we had met for lunch a couple of weeks after his wife had left. I remembered how devastated he was, how confused.

I realized that at that earlier time he was struggling with the change, the incomprehensible situation. And I saw that with time he had been able to take his mind off the change and to start to grapple with the transition. That is really common. When a person is overwhelmed by a change, the transition—and particularly the ending—is almost impossible to comprehend. That, in turn, reminds us that time not only reconciles us to loss but also helps us to *understand* the loss so that we can live through it. It is all the more unfortunate that our change-obsessed and transition-ignorant society keeps us trying to make sense of endings in the context of change rather than in the context of transition. For it is only in the context of the transition process that endings hold personal meaning and open the gate to our own transformation.

THE EXPERIENCE OF THE ENDING

Endings begin with something going wrong. At Ismaros, Odysseus failed where he had always succeeded before. At Thebes, Oedipus experienced a subtler and more pervasive loss—a deadening, a withering, a loss of vitality. For one person, an ending may be an event; for another, it may be a state of mind.

Nor do the elements in an ending come in any particular order. In a divorce, for example, one partner may experience disidentification and disorientation and then decide to act—which leads to disengagement. For the other partner, unaware of the impending change, the ending begins with disengagement and the challenge of disenchantment. There is no natural or normal order.

Nor is there a normal order of reactions to an ending. Some people react to endings the same way that Elisabeth Kubler-Ross found terminally ill patients reacting to their impending deaths: a five-stage sequence that moves from denial to anger to bargaining to depression to acceptance.[4] One can see that general course of response in Oedipus. But others seem to reverse this course by starting with apparent acceptance and discovering only much later that they have lost something in the transition.

The point is that it is important to let yourself or others in transition experience an ending. You are not the first person who ever lost a job (or moved or had heart surgery), but telling you that is of no help. If you keep fighting your experience, I can only conclude that you just can't let go of something in this process. You may well need help, perhaps professional help, but you don't need me to tell you to stop crying over spilt milk and put on a happy face.

Endings are, let's remember, experiences of *dying*. They are ordeals, and sometimes they challenge so basically our sense of who we are that we believe they will be the end of *us*. This is where an understanding of endings and some familiarity with the old passage rituals can be helpful. For as Mircea Eliade, one of the greatest students of these rituals, has written, "In no rite or myth do we find the initiatory death as something *final*, but always as the condition *sine qua non* of a transition to another mode of being, a trial indispensable of regeneration; that is, to the beginning of a new life."[5] Even though we are all likely to view an ending as the conclusion of the situation it terminates, it is also—and it is too bad that we don't have better ways of reminding ourselves of this—the initiation of a process. We have it backwards. Endings are the first, not the last, act of the play.

The Neutral Zone

I do my utmost to attain emptiness; I hold firmly to stillness. (XVI)
Do that which consists in taking no action; pursue that which is
not meddlesome; savour that which has no flavor. (LXIII)

—LAU TZU
Tao Te Ching[1]

IN OTHER TIMES AND PLACES, THE PERSON IN TRANSITION
left the village and went into an unfamiliar stretch of forest or
desert. There the person would remain for a time, removed from
the old connections, bereft of the old identities, and stripped of the
old reality. This was a time "between dreams" in which fundamen-
tal chaos of the world's beginnings welled up and obliterated all
forms. It was a place without a name—an empty space in the world
and the lifetime where a new sense of self could gestate.

One of the difficulties of being in transition in the modern
world is that we have lost our appreciation for this gap in the continuity of existence. For us, "emptiness" represents only the absence
of something. So when what's missing is something as important as
relatedness and purpose and reality, we try to find ways of replacing
these missing elements as quickly as possible. That state of affairs,
we imagine, cannot be an important part of the transition process;

we hope it can only be a temporary, if unfortunate, situation to be endured.

In this view, transition is seen as a kind of street-crossing procedure. One would be a fool to stay out there in the middle of the street any longer than was necessary; so once you step off the curb, you move on to the other side as fast as you can. And whatever you do, don't sit down on the centerline to think things over!

No wonder we have so much difficulty with our transitions. This view makes no sense out of the pain of ending, for we imagine that our distress is a sign that we should not have crossed the street in the first place. It also makes no sense of the feeling of lostness that we are likely to experience, nor of the feeling that the emptiness seems to stretch on forever. ("Wait a minute," we want to object. "There *is* another side to this street, isn't there?") And as for transition as a source of self-renewal, well, after you've struggled and floundered across a scary place like that, you *need* some self-renewal.

Yet even as we distort and misunderstand the neutral zone, we live it out unwittingly. Without quite knowing why, people in the middle of transition tend to find ways of being alone and away from all the familiar distractions. Perhaps it is a long weekend in a borrowed cabin by a lake, or perhaps it is a few days alone in a city hotel. One member of that first transition class had just returned from four days ("the strangest four days in my life," she called them) backpacking alone in the mountains. "Where can we reach you?" her husband asked with concern. The woman, who had never before gone anywhere by herself, replied simply, "You can't. But I'll be back."

Whenever they ask, we tell the people we are leaving behind that we just want to get away by ourselves for a little while—which is probably as much as we ourselves know at the time. Friends and family members may have their own anxious fantasies of what we are really doing—meeting a secret lover, going off to end it all, or abandoning them to begin life under a new identity elsewhere. (And we may very well be playing with one or more of these possibilities in our own fantasies.)

If we do tell people where we are going, they ask in genuine puzzlement, "What are you going to *do* there all alone?" We hardly know what to answer, though, for we are heading down a dark pathway in our lives. "I want time to think things over, I guess," we say a little lamely. But then it turns out that once we are out there, we don't really *think* in any way that produces definite results. Instead, we walk the beaches or the back streets. We sit in the park or the movie theater. We watch the people and the clouds. "I didn't do much of anything," we report upon our return. And we feel a little defensive, as though we had failed to deliver on our promise.

You should not feel defensive about this apparently unproductive time-out during your transition points, for the neutral zone is meant to be a moratorium from the conventional activity of your everyday existence. The activities of your ordinary life keep you "you" by presenting you with a set of signals that are difficult to respond to in any but the old way. Only in the apparently aimless activity of your time alone can you do the important inner business of self-transformation. But you don't *do* it as you do ordinary things, for it is in the walking, watching, making coffee, counting the birds on the phone wire, studying the cracks in the plaster ceiling over the bed, dreaming, and waiting for God-knows-what to happen that you are carrying on the basic industry of the neutral zone, which is attentive inactivity and ritualized routine.

In the old passage rituals, people were brought up and educated to know what to do in these natural but mysterious gaps in the lifetime. They learned to solicit the aid of dream figures, the so-called spirit guides of one sort or another. They were instructed in symbolic modes of perception wherein the natural order became a symbolic communication written for their enlightenment and guidance. They learned to cultivate mental states in which heightened kinds of awareness were possible—sometimes by means of meditation and chanting, sometimes through fasting and dehydration in the sweat-lodge, and sometimes with the aid of psychotropic substances.

A modern account of such instruction is given in Carlos Castaneda's books about Don Juan and his Yaqui teachings. Whether these are taken as fact or fiction, they represent an unusually rich account of a modern Westerner's encounter with the neutral-zone experience in its starkest and most powerful form. One finds descriptions of the teaching and the resulting experiences almost anywhere one opens the four books. I open the first at random and find this:

> Don Juan waited a while and then, going through the same motions, handed me the lizards again. He told me to hold their heads up and rub them softly against my temples, as I asked them anything I wanted to know. I did not understand at first what he wanted me to do. . . . He gave me a whole series of examples: I could find out about persons I did not see ordinarily, or about objects that were lost, or about places I had not seen. Then I realized he was talking about divination. I got very excited. My heart began to pound. I felt that I was losing my breath.[2]

Such ways of knowing are so alien to most of us that they seem bizarre and even frightening. But many ordinary members of our own culture have had similar experiences (often discounted or even denied afterwards) of extraordinary kinds of awareness in their own neutral zones. Lacking guidance and validation at such times, most people who have such experiences are frightened and troubled by them.

One of the members of the first transition class was a former electrical engineer named Pat, a man in his forties, who said little about himself except that he had "dropped out of the rat race," as he put it. Bit by bit, we discovered that he had been laid off by a space-industry firm; a few months later, he had separated from his wife after bitter disagreements about his lack of initiative in finding another job. "I didn't want to lose that job," he said one night, "but once it was gone, I realized that I didn't want another like it. I didn't know what I did want, and my wife found my indecisiveness too frustrating, so she left."

All this was said with so little feeling that one might have thought he was talking about someone else's life. But when he shifted to the subject of the present and his strange experiences, he came to life again. It seemed that his entire reality had changed. He had never dreamed much before, but now he was dreaming every night. He had had several experiences of "seeing," as he called it. "Seeing" meant really understanding what his life was all about and why he had lost his job and his marriage. "I feel as though I've broken through a wall and can see the world for the first time," he said with real feeling.

Some members of the class dismissed Pat as someone who'd gone off the deep end, but others said that they knew what he was talking about. His honesty made it easier for others to talk, and we soon discovered that the encounter with "another level of reality" was not uncommon in our group. Some chalked it up to a great activation of their imaginations, others to some new access to areas of their consciousness that they hadn't been aware of before, and a few argued for actual contact with spiritual presences. "You can say anything you want to about it," one woman said defiantly, "but I've found out that I have a guide that I can talk to when I get into the right frame of mind."

What we were discovering that night, and what too few people in transition have the opportunity to hear, is that for many people the breakdown of the old "enchantment" and the old self-image uncovers a hitherto unsuspected awareness. Not everyone in transition has this experience, but it is common enough to suggest that the old consciousness-altering techniques used in rites of passage did not *create* a different reality but *amplified or enhanced* the natural tendency to see and understand the world differently in the gap between one life phase and the next.

This is an important discovery, for too many people either deny this aspect of the neutral zone experience or else become overwhelmed by it. To deny it is to lose the opportunity it provides for an expanded sense of reality and a deepened sense of purpose. And to be overwhelmed by it is just as unfortunate, for you then have no way to integrate the experience with the rest of your life. Either way, the transition process fails to provide you with the enrichment that is one of its natural but almost forgotten gifts.

In taking the initiate into the wilderness and enervating him or her with fasting and fatigue, in suppressing the initiate's old consciousness with chanting and rhythmical movements, in enlivening the imagination with mythic tales and symbolic procedures of various sorts—in all these ways, traditional societies opened the person to the transformative experiences of the neutral zone. Furthermore, they made those experiences intelligible and capable of assimilation. With us, however, it's a hit-or-miss affair at best. We aren't sure what is happening to us or when it will all be over. We don't know whether we are going crazy or becoming enlightened, and neither prospect is one that we can readily discuss with anyone else.

For many people, the experience of the neutral zone is essentially one of emptiness in which the old reality looks transparent and nothing feels solid anymore. Leo Tolstoy left us with a powerful description of his own encounter with that nothingness: "I felt," he wrote, "that something had broken within me on which my life had always rested, that I had nothing left to hold on to, and that morally my life had stopped." He became obsessed with death and even gave up hunting for fear that he would turn his gun on himself one day. Outwardly, his life showed few signs of change:

> And yet I could give no reasonable meaning to any actions of my life. And I was surprised that I had not understood this from the very beginning, My state of mind was as if some wicked and stupid jest was being played upon me by someone. . . . [I asked myself] what will be the outcome of what I do today? Of what I shall do tomorrow? What will be the outcome of all my life? Why should I live? Why should I do anything?[3]

There, under the surface of his everyday life, Tolstoy had discovered the great emptiness of the neutral zone.

I sometimes wonder what would have happened if Tolstoy had brought his anguish to a conventional therapist—and I imagine exchanges like the following:

"When did you first notice this 'wicked and stupid jest,' as you call it?"

"I've felt it for weeks."

"Have you always suspected that people were making fun of you this way?"

Or: "How are things between you and Mrs. Tolstoy these days?"

Or: "Tell me something about your childhood."

Or, just as bad as these but more current: "Well, now, Leo—you don't mind if I call you Leo, do you?—we call these difficult times a 'mid-life crisis.'"

Perhaps Tolstoy was fortunate in having to do without the assistance of a psychoanalyst. All the same, he clearly could have used help—someone who could appreciate his suffering and his confusion, some way of making sense out of it, some route to follow through it. He could have endured his situation a little better, perhaps, if he had realized that the emptiness he was experiencing was the natural sequel to an inner ending and that the ending and the emptiness were simply the first two phases of a process that would (unless it was somehow aborted) provide him with a new sense of who he was and where he was going. He might have felt a little less alone if he had realized how common his experience was. And he could have faced the future more confidently if he had used some tools with which to clear a pathway through the wilderness.

These "tools" were once provided by the tribal elders in the form of instruction and ritual, but today we must fashion our own tools. It is tempting to think that we could recover and re-animate lost rituals, but that seldom works very well. Rather, we need to understand which neutral zone activities the old rituals were designed to facilitate and then discover our own ways of doing those things.

The first of the neutral zone activities or functions is *surrender*—one must give in to the emptiness and stop struggling to escape it. This is not easy, although it is made easier by an understanding of why the emptiness is essential. There are three main reasons for the emptiness between the old life and the new. First, the process of transformation is essentially a death and rebirth process rather than one of mechanical modification. Although our own culture knows all about mechanics, it has a great deal to learn from the past about death and rebirth. As Mircea Eliade has written, "For the archaic and traditional cultures, the symbolic return to chaos is indispensable to any new Creation."[4] In this sense, chaos is not simply "a mess." Rather, it is the primal state of pure energy to which the person (or an organization, society, or anything else in transition) must return for every true new beginning. It is only from the perspective of the old form that chaos looks fearful. From any other perspective, it looks like life itself, as yet unshaped by purpose and identification. But it is, of course, from that "old form" perspective that anyone who has just been plunged into transition views life, so it is no wonder that the neutral zone's emptiness and fluidity are frightening.

The second reason for the gap between the old life and the new is that the process of disintegration and reintegration is the source of renewal. As van Gennep noted in his seminal *Rites of Passage:*

> Although a body can move through space in a circle at a constant speed, the same is not true of biological or social activities. Their energy becomes exhausted, and they have to be regenerated at more or less close intervals. The rites of passage ultimately correspond to this fundamental necessity.[5]

In our age of stress, alienation, and burnout, this is surely a piece of wisdom that we need to recover. In keeping with our mechanistic bias, we have tried to make do with "recharging" and "repair," imagining that renewal comes through fixing something defective or supplying something that is missing. But it is only by returning for a time to the formlessness of the primal energy that renewal can take place. The neutral zone is the only source of the self-renewal that we all seek. We need it, just the way that an apple tree needs the cold of winter.

The last reason for the emptiness between the stages of the life journey is the perspective it provides on the stages themselves. Viewed from the neutral-zone emptiness, the realities of the everyday world look transparent and insubstantial; we can see that everything we ordinarily think of as reality is now an "illusion." Few of us can live in the harsh light of that wisdom continuously, but even when we return to the engagements and identifications of ordinary "reality," we bring back with us an appreciation of the unknowable ground beyond every image. The neutral zone provides access to an angle of vision on life that one can get nowhere else. And it is a succession of such views over a lifetime that produces wisdom.

You may think this is heavy stuff—and it is. All you wanted was a little help in climbing out of the strange crack between life's floorboards that you unexpectedly fell into. Well, first you've got to understand what you're doing there, and then you've got to see why it's important to stay there for a while—and *then* we can talk about what to do.

For "what to do" consists not of ways out but of ways in; that is, it involves ways of amplifying and making more real the essential neutral zone experience. The way in *is* the way out, as it happens. When the wheels spin in loose gravel, you need more weight. Tempting though it may be to wait for the experience to pass, it is one of those things that will stick around until it gets your attention. So here are some practical suggestions about how to find the meaning while in the neutral zone—and thus how to shorten the time you spend there.

Accept your need for this time in the neutral zone. Understand why you are in this situation, why your life seems to be stalled at the very time changes are taking place around you. Being able to make sense out of your experience at this time is very important, for otherwise the neutral zone can feel like a dead-end road. Understanding what the neutral zone is and why it is there can keep you from falling into one of the two snares that people—especially people upset with and anxious about the transition they are in—fall into when they are in the neutral zone. Let's call them the *traps of fast forward* and *reverse*.

People often ask whether there isn't some way to speed up transition, to get it over sooner; when they do, they are usually thinking of the time in the neutral zone when very little seems to be happening. As does any unfolding natural process, the neutral zone takes its own sweet time. "Speeding things up," hitting the *fast forward* button, is a tempting idea, but that only stirs things up in ways that disrupt the natural formative processes that are going on. Far from bringing you out of the neutral zone sooner, such tactics usually set you back and force you to start over again. Frustrating though it is, the best advice is to opt for the turtle and forget the hare.

At the same time, do keep moving. Because the opposite temptation—to try to undo the changes and put things back the way they were before the transition started—is equally misguided. That undoubtedly *was* an easier time than this *nonplace* you occupy now! But your life lacks a replay button. The transition that brought you to this place cannot be undone. Even putting things back "the way they were" is a misnomer, because back *then*, you hadn't had the experience of being plunged into transition. And that experience won't go away.

Find a regular time and place to be alone. People in transition are often still involved in activities and relationships that continue to bombard them with cues irrelevant to their emerging needs. Be-

cause a person is likely to feel lonely in such a situation, the temptation is to seek more and better contact with others; but the real
need is for a genuine sort of aloneness in which inner signals can
make themselves heard. Doing housework after the kids leave for
school or paperwork with the office door shut are not *being alone* in
the sense I am talking about.

The old passage rituals provided the person with this experience
of deep aloneness, often in a wilderness setting. (Interestingly, the
Hebrew word for the "wilderness" in which Jesus, Moses, and Buddha spent time during critical periods of their lives is the same word
that means "sanctuary." This unmappable "nowhere" was also, as
several of these heroes were explicitly told, *holy ground.*) Tradition-
ally, time spent in such "sanctuaries" was a continuous period; but
you may have to plan your time to accommodate your own life situation. One person manages that by getting up every morning forty-
five minutes ahead of the rest of the family and sitting quietly in the
living room with a cup of coffee. Another jogs regularly after work
for half an hour. Another plays cassettes of ocean sounds and tem-
ple bells on his car stereo whenever he drives alone. Still another
has cleaned out a little storage room off the upstairs hall and sits
quietly alone in there for an hour after supper.

Begin a log of neutral zone experiences. Lost in the welter of mo-
ment-to-moment incident, the important experiences of the neutral
zone are often difficult to recognize. But as you look back, at the
end of a day or a week, they may stand out, like a path through the
grass that was all but invisible as you walked it. The approach you
take to logging these experiences is important, however, because it
can easily degenerate into a trivial kind of diary keeping. What you
want to capture is a day or a week of your experience: What was *really* going on, or even what was "trying to happen?" What was your

mood? What were you thinking about, perhaps without realizing it, at the time? What puzzling or unusual things happened? What decisions do you wish you could have made? What dreams do you remember having?

"But you don't see," says the man who approaches me after the lecture. "I'm nowhere and I want to get somewhere. This neutral zone—there's nothing here to record." Yes, it is a paradox, I agree, to talk about emptiness and then to suggest that something there is worth noting. The point is that we need to resist the tendency to imagine that what is needed is external to our situation. As Ralph Waldo Emerson put it, "Every man's condition is a solution in hieroglyphic to those in inquiries he would put. He acts it as life, before he apprehends it as truth."[6] We need to translate the *hieroglyphic,* and in so doing to make sense out of what we are experiencing.

When you record your experience, you slow down and force yourself to put things into words. And out of the blur of your experience, shapes start to emerge. Don't let yourself be carried away with expectations of what you'll find. Once when I was doing this myself, I found I was so busy waiting for an *answer* to the question I thought my life was asking that I was missing the inner experience of my mind's cranking out "answer" after "answer" in hopes of giving me what I wanted—or *thought* I wanted. You may find, as I did, that the neutral zone's gift to you is a ringside seat where you can watch your own mind making up "realities." Once you've had that experience, you will find it harder ever again to take yourself and your sufferings quite so seriously.

Take this pause in the action of your life to write an autobiography. You, an autobiographer? Why you, why now? Because sometimes it is only when you see where you have been that you can tell where you are heading. Because reminiscence is a natural impulse whenever something has just ended, as though you cannot really terminate anything without reviewing it and putting it into order. Because recollection is likely to turn up some useful information about other transitions in your past. And because that "past" is an artifact from another time and probably needs revision.

What you call your *past* is a tiny portion of your actual living, a selection of situations and events that is supposed to account for the *present*. One of George Orwell's slogans in *1984* was "Who controls the present controls the past; who controls the past controls the future."[7] Beneath his cynicism (history was always being self-consciously "revised" in that world, you remember), Orwell is accurately noting that it is the present situation that makes a given past make sense—and that a given past suggests a particular future. Even when we set out to change the present, the past defines the possibilities and the limits of the change.

Thus it is important in times of transition to reflect on the past for several reasons—not least of which is that, from the perspective of a new present, the past is likely to look different. For the past isn't like a landscape or a vase of flowers that is just *there*. It is more like the raw material awaiting a builder.

Let's say you were born in Pittsburgh, you have two sisters, and your grandmother died in 1953—or was it 1954? Well, it was about the time your father took that long business trip (he brought back sweaters for each one of you, remember?), and your mother seemed depressed. When you ask your older sister about this, she remembers that your parents had a big fight just before your father left, and she wonders whether the trip wasn't really a separation. (How come that never occurred to you?)

Well, anyway, that makes it 1953, and . . . wait. Maybe they did separate, because you were sent off unexpectedly to visit your uncle that summer—and you almost stayed when they offered you the job at the coffee shop. Boy, that was a real crossroads in your life, although you didn't know it then. (What do you suppose would have happened if you *had* stayed and hadn't started college the next year?)

You can't follow the thread of your life very far before you find "the past" changing. Things that you haven't remembered in years reappear, and things that you've always thought were *so* turn out to be not so at all. If the past isn't the way you thought it was, then the present isn't, either. Letting go of that present may make it easier to conceive of a new future. Things look different from the neutral zone, for one of the things you let go of in the ending process is the need to see the past in a particular way, and in doing that you let go of the need to think of the future in the way you always have. Boy, once you start that, the possibilities begin to open up.

Take this opportunity to discover what you really want. What *do* you want, anyway? When the circumstances of our lives box us in, we usually assume that we know what we want but simply cannot get it. "If only I could . . ." The refrain is familiar. In times of transition, however, a distressing change often takes place: The limiting circumstances are part of what ends, and we are no longer held back from doing what we want to do. But now the refrain changes: "If only I knew what I really wanted . . . "

Wanting turns out to be a far less clear matter than we usually imagine, for it is overlayed with a lifetime of guilt and ambivalence. As children, we may have been told that we were selfish or that we were never satisfied with what we got. Or perhaps we were told that we only *thought* we knew what we wanted. ("You don't really want that. . . . When you're older, you'll realize. . . . You *really* want to please Mommy, don't you?") Or else the simple pain of disappointment grew too great as our wants were disregarded time after time, and we learned to protect ourselves by blocking off an awareness of our wantings.

So here you are now, in a position to get little of what you want after all these years, and you find yourself unsure and confused. How can you move past this difficulty and use your real wantings to orient you toward the future? By understanding how you characteristically suppress your wantings and how to stop doing that. To do these things, try this:

Imagine that you are going to get yourself something to eat or drink right now. (Assume for the moment that you can actually have anything you want—all the ordinary problems of cost and supply are taken care of.) Now, stop reading for just a moment and think: "What do I really want to eat or drink right now?" (Take one or two minutes to think about that before you read any further.)

What did you do with that question? Forget the answer that you did or did not come up with, and think instead about the answer-getting process. How did you go about it?

1. Did you consult your mouth or your stomach or your mind?
2. Did you try to *figure out* the answer as though it were a question on a history test?
3. Did you imagine a menu and run over the possibilities—hamburger, no . . . French fries, too greasy . . . ice cream, too fattening . . .
4. Did you try to remember something good you had eaten recently?
5. Did you try to recall your "favorite food"?
6. Did you come up with an answer and then shelve it because it was silly or strange?

Some people seem to know instinctively what they want, and they usually get their signals from their mouths or their stomachs. However, most people use some strategy to "come up with an answer." If you are one of those people, the chances are good that you do the same thing when it comes to far more important wantings about love and work or about what you're going to do next in your life. You get into serious difficulty when, in the neutral zone, you don't let yourself know what you really want out of your life. Remember, you don't have to *do* anything about the wanting; you just need be aware of it. It's overkill to control your behavior by denying that you're attracted to or interested in something.[8]

Think of what would be unlived in your life if it ended today. Suppose a tree fell on you right now or that you suffered heart failure. There. It's all over. Your life is finished. Whatever you've done is the *you* that goes down in the record books, and everything you might have done vanishes with the mind that considered it. Imagine that you are a family friend who has taken on the task of writing the obituary for the local paper or school alumni magazine. What would you write about yourself? Not your life story, but the things you did and didn't do with the years you had at your disposal. (You might actually write the obituary—it's a revealing exercise—but if you don't want to do that, at least pause for a few moments and jot down notes on a scrap of paper. You know the stuff: date of birth, parents and siblings, education, positions, honors, hobbies, and then some last sentence, "At the time of death he [she] was . . . " (Was what? Was groping toward a new beginning, was stuck, was miles from home with darkness falling, was running scared, was done with trying to meet the expectations of others at last . . . was what?)

Because endings are dyings in one sense, the obituary is an appropriate statement about your past. As you stand here in the emptiness of the neutral zone, what do you think and feel about the past? What was unlived in that past—what dreams, what convictions, what talents, what ideas, what qualities in you went unrealized? You are at a turning point now. The next phase of your life is taking shape. This is an opportunity to do something different with your life, something that expresses you in some significant way. This is a chance to begin a new chapter.

Take a few days to go on your own version of a passage journey. Several times I have said that it is impossible to reinstate the old rites of passage. Like transplants from an alien organism, they seldom "take" in a new setting. They are shaped by and for a sensibility that we have lost, and they depend on a lifetime of exposure to ceremonies and mental disciplines. Yet that does not mean that there is no way to mark or to dramatize your inner changes. As I have noted, you probably unwittingly do that already in taking time to be alone at transitional times in your life. I not am suggesting here that you learn about rituals and patch one together for yourself—only that you go a little further with the natural tendency to withdraw for a time during the neutral zone phase of transition. I am suggesting that you spend a few days alone during which you reflect consciously on the present transition process in your own life.

The place should be an unfamiliar one and free of the ordinary influences from your daily situation, as was the initiate's journey of old. The simpler and quieter the setting, the more chance you will have to attend to your inner business. Your food should be simple, and your meals should be small. Leave at home the wonderful novel you've been meaning to read, and don't distract yourself with other entertainment. Take along a notebook to jot in, but don't feel that you have to write anything substantial while you are there.

This retreat is a journey into emptiness and a time to cultivate receptivity. The more you leave behind, the more room you have to find something new. Do what you do attentively rather than distractedly while you wait for the *real* experience to come along. Making tea and putting on your shoes and watching a bird on the bush outside the window are the real experiences. Every detail is worth noticing—each is a note in the great symphony of peep-toot-and-boom.

If it appeals to you, keep a vigil during one of your nights—that is, stay awake all night and do nothing more demanding than keeping a fire going or getting something to drink occasionally. The idea is to stay awake, so you'll want to sit up rather than lie down, and it will help to get up and walk around from time to time.

There are no secrets to taking a neutral zone retreat, no great topics that you are supposed to meditate upon. You are simply living for a little while in a setting that corresponds to your position in life. You've removed the old reality glasses so that you can see the world anew. For this special time, take note of your hunches and the coincidences that happen and the crazy ideas that occur to you and the dreams that you remember for those first few seconds in the morning. If you think of small symbolic actions you could perform in this place, go ahead and do them. One person scratches out a design with a stick in the dust and then sits in the middle; another writes out a description of all that she has been trying to do in the last year and then burns it; another talks to the full moon; and still another carves strange spirals on the handle of a newfound walking stick. You can figure out what things mean later. For now, enter as fully as you can into whatever process is taking place.

A word of caution, though. The advice to participate in such a process is not an excuse to do foolhardy things. The midnight hike through the woods might leave you with a whopping case of poison oak or ivy. The lonely swim in the surf might cost you your life. This is a time for doing things that you wouldn't normally do, but it is not a time to hurt yourself.

Mostly it is a time to do whatever you do as though it were an element in an elaborate and ancient ritual and to do it with your total attention. For once in your life, you don't have to produce results or accomplish anything. If you are happy, be happy. If you are bored, be bored. If you are lonely or sad, be lonely or sad. There is not some better reaction you could be having to the experience. Whatever you are feeling is *you*, and you're there to be alone with that very person.

Since a life transition is a kind of buried rite of passage to begin with, your life will take on, willy-nilly, symbolic overtones at such times. The value of reflecting on the symbolism and making up little private rituals is not for the sake of ceremony but simply to become more aware of the shape of the natural transition process. Dying, the neutral zone, and rebirth are not ideas that we bring to life; they are phenomena that we find in life. The only trick is to see them by looking beyond the reflected light of the familiar surface of things and seeing what is really there working in the depths.

The neutral zone—the time between the old life and the new—is a particularly rich time for such insight. As I describe the transition process, I am conscious of simplifying it for the purposes of readier identification. I have been saying, for example, that the order of transition is ending, then neutral zone, then new beginning. But things do not stay lined up in their proper order in many people's lives. What I have been calling the in-between place of neutrality may actually precede a visible ending. Or it may come after a supposed beginning.

You see the former when someone "goes dead" at work or around the home. There has been no ending, no disengagement. The old job or the old relationship is intact. But the person is *not there*. He or she has become emotionally unplugged. Sometimes this happens because a decision has been made inwardly to end the situation. Emotionally, an ending has already taken place, although the outer circumstances remain unchanged. Or it may happen when you let go of an old dream because you finally admit to yourself that it is not going to work. Again, a subtle inner ending takes place, although everything goes on as before on the outside. The neutral zone overlaps with the old life, and you move like a sleepwalker through a role that you once identified with.

It often happens, however, that the external ending and the new beginning stand side-by-side with no room for a neutral space between them. You move from one town to another and the new life begins. Or from one job to another with no time off between them. Or a relationship begins, but there is no real ending to being alone. You are likely to be well into the new beginning before realizing that it is all strange and unreal. You probably say then that you "aren't used to the new situation yet," and it is true that things will seem less strange when the setting and the cues are more familiar. But it is also true that the strangeness comes from a belated encounter with the neutral zone.

Whether it overlaps with the old situation because inwardly some ending has already taken place, or whether it overlaps with the new situation because an inner new beginning has not yet been made, the neutral zone is a time of inner reorientation. It is the phase of the transition process that the modern world pays least attention to. By treating ourselves like appliances that can be unplugged and plugged in again at will or cars that stop and start with the twist of a key, we have forgotten the importance of fallow time and winter and rests in music. We have abandoned a system of dealing with the neutral zone through ritual, and we have tried to deal with personal change as though it were a matter of simple readjustment.[9]

In fact, the neutral zone is a time when the real business of transition takes place. It is a time when an inner reorientation and realignment are occurring, a time when we are making the all-but-imperceptible shift from one season of life to the next. Although such shifts cannot occur without an ending, and although they cannot bear fruit without a new beginning, it is in the neutral zone that the real work of transformation takes place. Looking back, people often say that "everything happened back then—even though, at the time, I didn't know what was going on." Also in retrospect, they will tell you that it was in the neutral zone (though they usually lack a name for the time) that they felt not only least sure what was going to happen but also most who-they-really-were. Or they will tell you these things if they have a way of making sense of what they are feeling and doing during this in-between time.

That is why it is such a misfortune that so few people can make sense out of the lostness and the confusion that they encounter when they have passed through those processes that start with *dis:* disengagement, dismantling, and disidentification. Without a key to that state, the resulting "disorientation" is viewed as no more than "confusion," and confused people imagine that they need to be straightened out or fixed. Without such a key, people in transition are like Alice at the bottom of the rabbit hole, muttering,

"It'll be no use their putting their heads down and saying, 'Come up again, dear!' I shall only look up and say, Who am I, then? Tell me that first, and then, if I like being that person, I'll come up: if not, I'll stay down here till I'm somebody else—but, oh dear!" cried Alice with a sudden burst of tears, "I do wish they would put their heads down! I am so *very* tired of being all alone here!"[10]

It *is* lonely down there—except that there are more people down there than you may realize.

As Arnold Toynbee pointed out, it is into some rabbit hole or cave or forest wilderness that creative individuals have always withdrawn on the eve of their rebirth. "The pattern of withdrawal and return," he called it, and he traced it out in the lives of St. Paul, St. Benedict, Gregory the Great, the Buddha, Muhammad, Machiavelli, and Dante.[11]

It is reassuring to find great figures groping through the darkness of the neutral zone, although we may still doubt that we will come across any burning bushes or that even a lifetime under a bo tree would produce enlightenment. Our own lives may be painted with a smaller brush, and our moments of discovery may be less grand— but the pattern is the same and it is even there in our own pasts, if we will look.

You Finish with a New Beginning

He has half the deed done, who has
Made a beginning.

—HORACE
Epistles[1]

IN THIS BOOK, AS IN THE TRANSITION PROCESS, we come to beginnings only at the end. It is when the endings and the time of fallow neutrality are finished that we can launch ourselves anew, changed and renewed by the deconstruction of the structures and outlooks of the old life phase and the subsequent journey through the neutral zone.

This simple truth goes against the grain of our mechanistic culture. We live in a world where things start with a switch or a key. If things don't start properly, we follow procedures to discover what is wrong. For something is surely wrong—mechanisms are made to start when we want them to.

These assumptions even influence the way in which we deal with that primal beginning, childbirth. Although evidence shows that attitudes are changing, birth has usually been regarded in this country as a surgical procedure, and pregnancy as a form of disability. The baby was taken and the mother put to sleep while the technicians did their work. The implications of these attitudes are far reaching, for as a society views birth, so it will view rebirth. Just as our primal beginning is mechanized, so are all subsequent beginnings; they are viewed as occasions for getting things started again after they have stopped. Without fully realizing it, we tend to imagine that "psychological obstetricians" can get us out, whack us on the back, and get us functioning again. Even as you start reading this chapter about the new beginning, you may well be waiting for the procedure that must surely be here somewhere—the checklist that you're supposed to run through when life has stalled and refuses to start up again properly.

I appreciate the difficulty, for I've struggled with it myself for most of my life. How do I know (I always wonder) when the ending is complete and when I've been in the neutral zone long enough? How do I know which path before me represents a genuinely new beginning or which footprints represent a real path—or even which marks in the dust represent real footprints? It's all very well to talk about new phases of life, but they're not different colors, the way the states were on our grammar school maps. There are times when I long for a simple way out, a procedure to follow rather than a process to understand.

But my life, and yours, goes forward regardless, and even as we look in vain for ways to get the machinery going again, we are doing unwittingly much of what we need to do to be renewed and changed. We forget how indirect and unimpressive most new beginnings really are, and we imagine instead some clear conscious steps that we ought to be taking. The English novelist John Galsworthy was surely right when he wrote that "the beginnings . . . of all human undertakings are untidy."[2]

Think back to the important beginnings in your own past. You bumped into an old friend that you hadn't seen for years, and he told you about a job at his company that opened up just that morning. You met your spouse-to-be at a party that you really hadn't wanted to go to and that you almost skipped. You learned to play the guitar while you were getting over the measles, and you studied French because the Spanish class met at 8:00 A.M. and you hated to get up early. You happened to pick up the book that changed your life simply because it was the only one lying on your friend's coffee table when you dropped by for an unexpected visit—and later you were astonished to find that you had once tried to read it before, but had put it aside as dull and confusing.

The lesson in all such experiences is that when we are ready to make a new beginning, we will shortly find an opportunity. The same event could be a real new beginning in one situation and an interesting but unproductive by-way in another. The difference is whether the event is "keyed" or "coded" to that transition point, the way that electronic key cards are set to open a particular hotel room door. When the card code matches, the door opens and the whole thing happens as if it were scripted. When it doesn't match, the event is just an event and you are still in the neutral zone. The neutral zone simply hasn't finished with you yet.

What isn't finished is the inner realignment and renewal of energy, both of which depend on your being immersed in the chaos of the neutral zone. It is as though the thing that you call "my life" had to return occasionally to a state of pure energy before it could take a new shape and gain new momentum. This is why in archaic cultures the myths describing the creation of the world are recited over a sick person. As Mircea Eliade has written:

By making the patient symbolically . . . contemporary with Creation, he lived again in the initial plentitude of being. One does not repair a worn-out organism, it must be re-made; the patient needs to be born again; he needs, as it were, to recover the whole energy and potency that a being has at the moment of its birth.[3]

No wonder it makes such a difference how a culture views birth, but it is also no wonder that we long for a way of avoiding the pain and struggle that rebirth requires.

Therefore, much as we long for external signs that point the way to the future, we must settle for inner signals that alert us to the proximity of new beginnings. The most important of these signals begins as a faint intimation of something different, a new theme in the music, a strange fragrance on the breeze. Because the signal is very subtle, it is difficult to perceive when other stimuli are strong—and that is why we naturally, if unconsciously, seek emptiness and quietness in times of life transition. This first hint may take the form either of an inner idea or of an external opportunity, its hallmark being not a logical sign of validity but the "resonance" it sets up in us.

With many of the people in transition that I've known, this first hint came in the form of an "idea" or an "impression" or an "image." There is no one word for the experience, but it involves imagining a scene or activity and feeling attracted to it. You could be doing that already without being aware of it, for the experience takes place right at the lower edge of consciousness—something like a half-formed daydream. One of the women in that original transition seminar had been imagining herself working with disturbed children for several years without realizing that this was something she wanted to do. One of the men in the class had a business venture planned out in fantasy, again without ever having acknowledged to himself that it represented a potential next step in his life.

Sometimes the hint comes in the form of a comment that somebody drops and that you find yourself remembering. "You depend so much on research," a friend told an aspiring writer that I knew, "but the things I like best in your writing come from your own experience." The remark was one of those reactions that one might easily forget, but this man could not forget it: "It nagged away at me," he said, "as though it were the answer to all my confusion—although it took me a year to see what the answer really meant."

Sometimes, the hint comes in the form of a dream. That should remind us how often traditional cultures taught their people to watch their dreams for signs of guidance. One member of the transition class had long been playing with the idea of doing something more serious with her skill as a weaver. "Place mats at Christmas are nice, but I have the feeling that it's not enough," she said. Then she dreamed she went home and, once inside the house, she found a strange corridor stretching out to the left where, in reality, there was only a blank wall. She went down the corridor, then down some stairs, and finally found herself in a small underground bedroom that apparently belonged to a small girl. She was astonished that she hadn't known about this room in her house before, but something about it was very appealing to her and she wondered who lived in it. "I wish it had been a studio or an art gallery," she said as we discussed the subject of dreams and guidance. It was only much later, when other signs had pointed her in that direction, that she recognized that her own childhood fantasy world was what she wanted to depict in tapestried images—and thus she began a career as a serious and successful tapestry maker.

This woman, like most of us, was looking too literally at the signs her life was providing her. She wanted to be an artist and she expected a signal, *yea* or *nay*. She wanted an "answer," like someone giving her a set of paints, and so she almost overlooked seeing that she was being given a path to follow. It was almost as though her dream had said, "Don't *be* something, *do* something." It was only when she stopped trying to be the artist that she began to explore the strange corridor in her life that she had never noticed before and found in the half-buried world of the little girl a way of looking at things that unlocked her natural talent and aligned her with her future.

Genuine beginnings depend upon this kind of inner realignment rather than on external shifts, for it is when we are aligned with deep longings (the real wantings discussed in Chapter 5) that we become powerfully motivated. Again and again, I have watched with amazement as people who are motivated in this way overcome what I would have taken to be insuperable obstacles to reach their goals. A woman of forty, for example, just divorced, the mother of three children, one of them seriously handicapped. With no college education, she had every reason to settle for the immediate solution of office work at a low salary. But she wanted to be a college teacher! "That will take *years*," everyone warned her. But one step at a time, she followed a path that led her through college, graduate school, a frustrating period of temporary jobs, and finally to the teaching job she had dreamed of.

Or the doctor in his forties who had always wanted to be a percussionist in a symphony orchestra. As a college student, he had been diverted by family pressure from following such an "impractical" dream, but now at fifty he had lived out their plan for him and had accumulated a modest fortune in real estate. He was in a com-

fortable rut, doing things mechanically and wondering at the emptiness of his life. A friend's daughter went to a music school one summer and played in the orchestra there, and he found himself imagining that he might do the same thing. The next year, he arranged to
take a month off and he did attend the summer school. The impact
was astounding. By the end of the month, his mind was made up.
The shift wasn't easy, however, for his life had to be rebuilt econom-
ically. It meant different kinds of investments, a smaller house, a new
loan to finish paying off the kids' college tuition. It also meant the
complicated process of terminating patients and disengaging himself
from active practice—not to mention devoting many hours to lessons and auditions and practice. But he did it, against the advice of
family and friends who said that he'd miss the affluence and excitement. "And I do miss them sometimes," he said, the last time I
talked to him, "but I've also never been happier."

I emphasize vocational changes in these examples because it is
when things come down to money and time that people always say
they just can't manage to launch the new beginning they dream of.
Examples of this sort are much commoner that most people realize,
for until recently the image of the linear lifetime and the linear career has so dominated our outlook and defined our expectations
that we have underestimated how often people do make radical
new beginnings during adulthood. Nor have we realized how often
important accomplishments come from such turning points.

We all learned in school, for example, about Abraham Lincoln's
youth—the poverty and the ambition and the sense of responsibility he had as a frontier boy. The history books imply that our greatest president was shaped by his childhood. But that childhood produced a young adult who was unremarkable—a man who did this
and that, and had a difficult marriage, a mediocre term in Con-

gress, and terrible bouts of what today would be diagnosed as depression. It was not from boyhood but from a profound transition in his thirties that this man stepped forth into history. It was only then that he discovered where he was going and what he could really do. Out of a dark time in his own inner neutral zone, Lincoln found the seeds of his future; and from there he began a rapid rise to the presidency that no one could have predicted for him only a few years earlier.

Gandhi, Eleanor Roosevelt, Mother Teresa of Calcutta, Walt Whitman—the names of famous people who began anew in the midst of adult life transitions are plentiful. Some discovered what they really wanted and then made their changes; others found life taking the lead and only subsequently found in transitions that they didn't want to make the opportunities to do what they seem to have been destined to do.

But there is a danger in citing too many of these examples, for it suggests that only great people or unusually talented ones can follow the path of self-renewal through transition; it suggests that only special people can make new beginnings during the adult years. And because such people became so successful, it is easy to imagine that the doubts and confusions we feel when we are trying to make a new beginning are significant evidence of bad timing, lack of potential, or having taken a wrong direction.

The truth is otherwise, and anyone who is trying to launch a new beginning needs to understand that. New beginnings are accessible to everyone, and everyone has trouble with them. Much as we may wish to make a new beginning, some part of us resists doing so as though we were making the first step towards disaster. Everyone has a slightly different version of these anxieties and confusions, but in one way or another they all arise from the fear that real change destroys the old ways that we have learned to equate to "who we are" and "what we need." To act on what we really want is the same as saying that "I, a unique person, exist." It is to assert that we are on our own in a much deeper sense than we ever imagined when we were originally setting up shop as adults. That earlier process involved only independence; this involves autonomy and the firm individual purpose on which that is based.

The great people point the way for us; but in the name of being role models for the rest of us, they often cover up the evidence of their confusion. When Eleanor Roosevelt looked back on her own painful life transition at thirty-five, she wrote, "Somewhere along the line of development we discover what we really are, and then we make our real decision for which we are responsible. Make that decision primarily for yourself because you can never really live anyone else's life, not even your own child's."[4] What she did not say was that her discovery came only after a terrible time of disenchantment and disorientation that almost killed her. She had discovered that her husband was having an affair with one of her most trusted friends. It was out of the shattered dream of domestic safety that she emerged, struggling against her own shyness and self-doubt, to become the important public figure in her own right that she remained for the rest of her life.

To make a successful new beginning, it is important to do more than simply persevere. It is important to understand what it is within us that undermines our resolve and casts doubt on our plans. One member of the transition class was close to the truth when he said, "There's a tough old immigrant inside me who is scared to death of anything new and who believes that the only way to survive is to do everything the old, slow, safe way." This man was a scientist whose parents were immigrants who had lived out their lives in the narrow corridors of a city ghetto. Although he had made many external changes, he still lived by the safety code that they had taught him in childhood. No chances—take no chances. His life was a spider's web of precautions, and he picked up every threat to his life system through subtle vibrations along the strands.

Then came his transition. It was marital difficulty—his wife began to feel like a fly in the web—but it might just as well have been related to work or health or finances. Being reasonable, this man could see the changes he had to make. He could even feel the excitement of a new and less restrictive relationship with his wife. "In holding her less tightly, I'd free myself, too," he said. "The guard is a prisoner too, you know."

But each step forward set off an inner warning system, and he would retreat in confusion to the old ways of being. One day, he was ready to launch a new life, and the next he was bitterly suspicious about the motives of others and his own promptings. "What am I trying to prove?" he would ask belligerently. "My life's not so bad as it is!" and then he would go through a time of resisting change and undermining the temptation to go for what he really deeply wanted at that point in his life—more freedom, more energy, new goals.

This man finally decided to go into psychotherapy, for his inner resistance to transition was too great for him to deal with on his own. For many people, however, that is not so. Identifying their inner resistance and understanding the symptoms of its activity is enough. They find that this inner reactionary (as one woman called it) is stirring up trouble in a relationship. She found herself being unwittingly belligerent or provocative, almost as though she was trying to start a fight so that she could say, "There, that proves it. He won't let me change." Or such people may find themselves plung-

ing unexpectedly into a depression at the prospect of a new beginning—and find on closer examination that the inner reactionary is
muttering, "All right, if you won't do what I say, I'll bring this show
to a standstill." Or they may find themselves getting confused and
forgetting what they want, as if the inner reactionary were saying,
"So you won't pay any attention to my warnings, huh? OK, then, I'll
fog up your brain so that you won't remember where you are, and
then you'll have to cancel that big trip you're planning."

It is as though each of us had some inner figure whose idea of
caring for us involved only taking us into protective custody whenever we threatened in the transition process to become too autonomous. Some people find the figure activated whenever risk is
involved; others experience the inner sabotage whenever they try to
come in from the cold and settle down. One person's safety involves
inactivity and another's involves perpetual motion; but either way, a
new beginning upsets a long-standing arrangement.

The same thing happens externally in relationships, where new
beginnings often bring conflict and even a sense of betrayal. The
person's imminent change sets off danger signals in the other, for it
rightly suggests that the old tacit agreements on which the relationship was based are headed for renegotiation. "You be this way and
I'll be that way" doesn't work any more, because now *I* want to be
that way and you . . . well, you will have to do some changing, too.
A situation such as this must be dealt with openly and honestly, for
indirection and denial only increase the other's resistance.

It is important to distinguish between a real new beginning in
someone's life and a simple defensive reaction to an ending. Each
may exert strain on a relationship, but the new beginning must be
honored. The defensive reaction is simply a new way of perpetuating the old situation and needs to be considered as such.

On the second or third meeting of the transition class, for example, one of the men arrived in a state of bitterness and frustration. His forty-year marriage was on the rocks, he said, and it was all because his wife could not adjust to his recent retirement. He began to think that she just wanted him for a paycheck, he said with heavy sighs, and now that he was there as a person, she didn't really care for him.

We were well into a state of commiseration when someone asked him exactly what had happened to show him this side of his wife. It turned out that he had reorganized the kitchen for her, and she had kicked him out of the house. A very precise and orderly man who had been used to supervising others, he discovered in the empty first days of his new leisure a fresh field for his talents—the kitchen cupboards. His wife had come home from a trip to the city to find everything in the kitchen in a new place, a neat label on each shelf and a list on the back of each cupboard door. "Look what I got for trying to help her," he said bitterly.

This man honestly believed that his actions were part of the transition process. ("I never *used* to help around the house before," he said.) He claimed that his wife couldn't stand to see him change. However, it was *he* who couldn't stand to change—or rather to go through the three-phase transition process to a new beginning. Instead, he was just perpetuating his old style and activity in a new way. He was avoiding an ending and calling the result a new beginning.

Unfortunately, there is no psychological test you can take at such times. It is often difficult to be sure whether some path leads forward or back, and it may be necessary to follow it for a little way to be sure. But there are two signs that are worth looking for before you start. The first is the reaction of people who know you well: not whether they approve or disapprove, but whether they see what you propose to do as something new or simply a replay of an old pattern. The second indication comes from the transition process itself: Have you really moved through endings into the neutral zone and found there the beginning you now want to follow, or is this "beginning" a way of avoiding an ending or aborting the neutral zone experience?

Genuine beginnings begin within us, even when they are brought to our attention by external opportunities. It is out of the formlessness of the neutral zone that new form emerges and out of the barrenness of the fallow time that new life springs. We can support and even enhance the process, but we cannot produce the results. Once those results begin to take shape, however, there are several things that can be done.

The first, very simply, is to stop getting ready and to act. "Getting ready" can turn out to be an endless task, and one of the forms that inner resistance can often take is the attempt to make just a few more (and then more, and again more) preparations. It is true, of course, that timing is important in a new undertaking. (You may remember trying again and again to lose weight or stop smoking or start jogging—and then one day you discover that it seems to happen almost by itself.) Yes, until you are really ready, you probably won't make a real beginning. But that does not mean that your odds are improved by complicated steps taken to "get ready." When the time comes, stop getting ready to do it—and do it!

The second thing you can do is to begin to identify yourself with the final result of the new beginning. What is it going to feel like when you have actually done whatever it is that you are setting out to do? All right, then, say it's done. There, you did it. You are the person who does that sort of thing. People look at you now as "the-one-who-did-it," and by seeing yourself through their eyes, you real-ize what self-confidence is: experiencing yourself as one who can do things like that. You can see that your way of looking at other people endows them with the special power or ability to do things that you used to think you lacked. Their specialness and difference from you was a mantle that you laid over their shoulders, and you can take it back now and wear it yourself.

I often go through this routine myself at the beginning of a new project. (You'd think I'd learn and not keep making the same old self-defeating mistakes over and over, but I don't ever seem to get it, once and for all.) Let's say that I am trying to convince a group of executives that their plan for a big organizational change is unreal-istic from a transition point of view. They are full of enthusiasm about the change they want to make and don't want to hear that they are heading for trouble. As I start talking about transition, they look at me skeptically, as if to say, "Who *is* this guy, and what is he talking about?" As they squint down the long table at me, I feel as though I am *nobody* talking to *somebody*. Who am I to tell them what to do? I am afraid that I sound like someone saying, "I know that you have your plans all set, and I know that you think that *you* are the real pros here, but let me ask you (please) to take a minute to consider . . . "

Then I get a grip on myself and recall what it feels like when an executive team does study its plans with transition in mind and how wonderful it is when a well-made transition plan helps them to fore-see and avoid the resistance that fouls up so many organizational changes. I remember what it is like to be sharing a feeling of ac-complishment with them and hearing that my warnings helped them avoid costly delays and disruptions. I'm really offering them (I tell myself) the best way to achieve the results that they really want.

What I am urging is really a wonderful opportunity for them, not only to succeed but to learn something new in the process. I take a deep breath. "I want to suggest something that I think will help you get the results you are after," I say and my voice sounds different now, even to me. I imagine how lucky they are to have dealt with their problem in advance, how much money and time they have saved. I'm really doing them a *huge favor*, I think.

Such strategies have only a temporary effect, and they do no good if the thing I am recommending is not something that I believe in wholeheartedly. And even when it is, there will be times of losing momentum, times when my inner reactionary says, "Look at them eyeing you skeptically. They doubt you. There must be a lot of places you'd rather be right now—besides this conference room. How about tossing in the towel and wishing them good luck with a project you know is going to bomb—but that you won't be blamed for? You *warned* them, after all." I feel all these things, but I also know enough about my own resistance to transition to see how important it is to continue with the transition process.

This is where the third thing to do is important: Take things step by step and resist the siren song that sings about some other route where everything goes smoothly and events are always exciting and meaningful. In making a beginning, you can become so invested in the results that whatever you have to do to reach them looks pretty insignificant. Trudging from appointment to appointment, licking stamps, adding columns of figures, making reminder phone calls, and explaining your idea for the hundredth time—these are the trivia from which vital new ventures finally emerge. But by comparison with the goal, they seem hopelessly dull.

In an important new beginning, a preoccupation with results can be damaging. There was a vocational counselor in the transition class who had recently moved to our area and was looking for a new job. He had given himself three months to find it, but before a month was out he reported that he wasn't making it. Every interview that did not produce a job became a *failure* and everything he said had been, he suspected, a *mistake.*

It was only when he shifted his attention from the intended goal to the process of investigation that he lost this sense of discouragement—and, not coincidentally, I think, found a job quickly. Instead of seeing the interviews as shots at a target (damn, missed again!), he saw them as strands in a complex web of activity. Each interview taught him something or created a new contact or deepened his understanding of himself. He saw himself as searching and learning rather than as "not finding what he was after." And in the process, he learned the fourth important thing to remember in making a beginning, which is to shift your purpose from the goal to the process of reaching the goal.

This advice is not simply a way of checking your disappointment when your progress is slow. It also represents the real mechanics of the transition process—which is a process, after all, and not a three-positioned switch. Even though the external "new beginning" may happen very quickly once it becomes evident, the internal re-identification and re-engagement always occur more slowly. Many of the old passage rituals recognized this fact by bringing the renewed person back from the neutral zone in several steps and over time—a few days or weeks being spent in a couple of "halfway houses" along the way back to the village.

Like so much else about the transition process, we have lost the social mores that once structured beginnings. But we can nevertheless draw on that lore to act wisely and considerately on our own behalf and in our treatment of others. It is unrealistic to expect someone to make a beginning like that of a sprinter coming out of the starting blocks. Even when your outer situation is complete—you're on the new job, you're finally married, you're in your new house—the inner beginnings are still going on. At such a time, people often say, "I guess I'm just not used to this new situation yet," but it would be more accurate to say that "I'm not quite fully the new person yet—but I'm getting there." It is a time to be gentle with yourself or with the other person, a time for the little supports and indulgences that make things easier. And it is a time to acknowledge that, as much as we long for them, new beginnings can be things to be resisted just as much as the loss-filled ending and the ambiguous and frustrating neutral zone were.

Not everything vanishes in the ending process, of course, and some people find it important to experience the continuities in their lives when so much else is changing. I am typing these words right now at my dining room table, for example, a table that my parents bought before I was born, a table that I ate all my childhood meals on, a table that represents to me that the New England world I came out of is my background. And now, living in California, where I raised my children very differently from the way I was raised and where I directed my life toward goals that are quite different from those with which I started, I find real pleasure in knowing that some of the important new beginnings that I have made in the past quarter century have involved working on this piece of furniture that is old and dear to me.

It is, after all, a new chapter of *my* life that is beginning. I haven't become somebody else. The beginning isn't happening to some "him" who rose up new and complete. The transition process is really a loop in the life journey, a going out and away from the main flow for a time and then a coming around and back. The neutral zone is meant to be only a temporary state. It is, as they say, a great place to visit, but you wouldn't want to live there. When the neutral zone has done its work, you come back.

Socially, this means that the isolated person returns from the disengaged state and the wilderness to set about translating insight and idea into action and form. This return may take the form of new commitments at home and at work: The person is really *there* again after a time of being somewhere else. The same return may take the person into new relationships or projects. But either way, the old connections that were broken with the earlier disengagement are there to be reattached, greatly modified though they may be.

Psychologically, the process of return brings us back to ourselves and involves a reintegration of our new identity with elements of our old one. This connection is necessary if we are going to be grounded and not "up in the clouds." This aspect of the beginning is as natural as the *dis*integration was back in the termination phase. Inwardly and outwardly, one *comes home*. As a wonderful Zen saying expresses it, "After enlightenment, the laundry."

Endings and beginnings, emptiness and germination in between: That is the shape of the transition periods in our lives, and these times come far more frequently in adulthood and cut far more deeply into it than most of us imagined they would. But the same process is also going on continuously throughout our lives. As humankind once knew and celebrated, it is the same rhythm that puts us to sleep at night and wakes us in the morning after a dark time full of half-remembered and enigmatic clues. It is what carries us through the turning year to an ending that opens to yet another new beginning. And so it is with our lives—a dozen little endings, hardly noticed in the day-to-day rush, plunge us into little wildernesses; and a dozen little beginnings take shape in confusion and emerge unexpectedly into clear form. ("Where did *that* idea come from?" "When did you decide that?")

Endings and beginnings, with emptiness and germination in between. That basic shape is so essential to growth that we must learn to recognize it in our lives. The societies that were most knowledgeable about it and designed rituals to facilitate it had, however, little faith in descriptions. Literal statements do not reach deep enough in the mind to have a lasting effect. For that reason, these societies couched their most important insights in the form of stories. That is why I retold the tale of Oedipus and the riddle of the sphinx, and why I recounted the story of Odysseus and the homeward journey. To summarize the basic transition process, I'd like to turn to another story: that of Amor and Psyche.

EPILOGUE

Once upon a time—which is to say, right now and from the beginning and till the end—there was a very lovely young woman. She was the loveliest woman in the kingdom, but although this was universally admitted, no one courted her. Others married and began families, but Psyche (for that was her name) seemed too perfect for any ordinary mortal.[2]

Psyche's parents finally sent to the great oracle at Delphi for an answer, and the answer came back. But when they heard it, they wept, for the oracle said that Psyche must die. She was to be dressed in funeral clothes and taken to a wild and desolate crag in the mountains on the far side of the kingdom. There she was to be abandoned.

In stories one does not ask why, for everything goes according to a plan that is patterned on life itself. The oracle is saying that no new time of life is possible without the death of the old lifetime. To gain, you must first give up.

So they dressed Psyche in funeral clothes and conducted her death rites and left her on the cold and windy mountaintop. As she lay there, numb with fear and sunk in despair, Amor, the god of passionate love, came to her side. Gazing on her perfection, he fell in love with her. He flew off to bring the West Wind, his helper, and to ask him to carry Psyche down into the hidden valley beneath the mountain tops where Amor lived in a dark palace.

So it was that when she awoke, Psyche found herself in a mysteriously beautiful castle. Everything she could possibly need was there—food and drink, lovely clothing, perfumed baths, everything but companionship. But then when darkness fell, she found that she had that, too, for Amor came to her in the darkness and slept with her. Night after night he did this. Sometimes they talked all night, sometimes they made love, and sometimes they dined together in the darkness and fell asleep at once. Psyche could not have asked for more. She was happy at last.

As always happens, an ending clears the ground for a new beginning. In this story, the person did little—everything just happened. Some transitions are like that. They just happen. But when they happen this way, something is missing. The outer situation has taken shape, but the inner state remains unchanged. The old outlook, the old self-image, the old value system remain intact. Outwardly, the change is complete, but the real transition process has hardly begun.

In time, Psyche began to feel a strange incompleteness about her life. Everything was perfect, but she missed her old friends and her family. This hidden palace was indeed beautiful, but it was also unreal—outside the real world, outside time, outside human connections. She talked of this to her secret lover. She told him she wished to see her family again. Could her sisters come and visit her, perhaps?

Amor at first refused, but she longed so for contact with her family that he at last relented. They must come, he said, when he was away, and they must be gone before his return. She was delighted and promised to do as he said.

The sisters came, carried by the same West Wind that had brought Psyche to this paradise. They were amazed—and jealous. Who was this secret lover, they asked? Psyche did not know, of course, but she made up stories. (She had never seen him because he came in the darkness and never showed her his face.) Psyche hid her ignorance as well as she could, but it was not long before her answers began contradicting one another. "You don't even know what he looks like!" cried the sisters. "Why, he is probably a great beast that uses the darkness to hide his awful ugliness! You have been a fool. You have a wicked and loathsome animal for a lover."

When they left, Psyche was desperate with confusion. Amor seemed like a gentle, loving person. But it was true that he never let her see him. Her sisters' suspicion filled her head, and she vowed to find out the truth for herself. Late that night, after he had fallen asleep, she crept out and found a candle and a knife. She would steal a look at him, and if he were the terrible creature her sisters said he must be, she would stab him.

She lit the candle in the hall, and tiptoed up to the bed where he slept. Raising the candle in one hand and the knife in the other, she leaned over the bed. There he lay, the handsomest of gods! Amor, her lover. In her excitement, her hand trembled and hot wax fell onto the sleeping god's shoulder. He awoke. When he saw what she had done, he told her that, having broken the rule of darkness, she would never see him again. Suddenly he was gone, and Psyche was alone, stunned by what she had done and its effect.

In the everyday world of fact, agreements are meant to be kept, but in the world of myth everything happens for a reason and points to-ward some further end. Losses happen because it is time to let go of that way of being connected. Psyche had lived in the darkness for long enough, and it was now time for her to see. Yet the change was a violation of the old rules, and it destroyed the old situation. It was time for her to change—to grow and deepen, to take responsibility for who and where she was. It was time for the inner changes to catch up with the outer ones.

So Psyche left the palace where she had been so happy and began a lonely journey in search of her lost lover. In her grief, she called upon the gods for help, and one of them, the great Aphrodite, answered. "You seek my son," she said, for she was the mother of Amor, "but I think that you are not strong enough to do what must be done." Psyche said that it was not so; she would do anything.

"Very well. You must complete four difficult tasks," said Aphrodite. "First, you must sort out this roomful of seeds—put each type of seed in a separate pile—in one night." She threw open the door, and there Psyche saw a large room piled high with all kinds of seeds jumbled together in one immense heap. She gasped at the impossibility of the task, but Aphrodite continued without pause. "Second, you must go to the field where the golden-fleeced rams live—and bring me back some of that fleece." Psyche was stunned, for those rams breathed fire and killed anyone who entered their field. "And third," Aphrodite said before Psyche had time to recover, "You must bring me back a goblet of water from the great river—the River Styx—that plunges off the inaccessible cliffs and into the underworld." She looked at Psyche, amused by the hopeless look on the mortal's face.

"And finally," she said, "you must go down into hell itself and ask Persephone for a little box of her magic ointment that enhances one's beauty miraculously. Get it and bring it back to me." And having said that, Aphrodite vanished.

Psyche was stunned. Sadly, she opened the door and gazed at her first task. The pile of seeds was higher than her head, and it covered the floor of a good-sized room. She bent over and picked up a handful of seeds. Little ones, big ones, dark ones, light ones—no one could possibly bring order to this confusion in a year of sorting, and she had one night! The enormity of her task overcame her, and she sank down weeping at the edge of the pile. Feebly, she picked over a handful or two, but she was weary and depressed, and soon she fell asleep.

The first time her life had changed, Psyche had been quite passive—it had all just happened to her. Now, however, she was ready to act—but the tasks! They were impossible ones! She tried to do them, but then she had to give up. And when she did, she discovered that . . .

As she slept, a vast army of ants came into the room. On the command of their leaders, they began the sorting. All night they swarmed over the huge pile, and gradually it melted away until in its place were a dozen smaller piles of wheat and rye and beans and mustard seeds. At sunrise, Aphrodite threw open the door and woke the sleeping Psyche. Both of them gasped in amazement when they saw the piles of seed. Psyche said nothing, and Aphrodite said only, "You have three more tasks."

With the golden fleece and the water from the Styx, similar things happened. Just as she was about to give up hope of getting the fleece, the reeds that grew by the river whispered to her that if she waited until sunset when the rams retreated to their night's rest, she could creep up to the edge of the field and find bits of the fleecy treasure on the bushes. And just as she was about to abandon hope of getting a goblet of Styx water, a great eagle flew down from the heavens, took the vessel from her hands, and filled it from the torrent far above her head. Aphrodite was startled each time by Psyche's success, but she only said ominously, "We'll see how you do with the journey to the underworld."

What are the ants and reeds and the eagle? Why does something appear to help Psyche each time she has given up hope? The "helpful creature" is a common element in folklore and dreams, and it corresponds to some instinctive and subrational level of insight and energy. The tasks of transition are not, it seems, of the sort that one can consciously set out to accomplish. Yet neither are they taken care of in the automatic fashion of Psyche's original and outer transition on the mountaintop. Now she must struggle and even exhaust herself before help arrives—almost as though it is only when one is at the end of one's resources that new and hitherto unsuspected powers appear.

But, now, how is she to go to the underworld, survive its dangers, and return with the treasure? As she is on the verge of giving up, a tower near which she is standing begins to speak to her. It gives her instructions—bring coins to pay for her passage across the Styx, carry sweet cakes to pacify the guardian animals, and resist all requests from anyone for help. So off she goes. The coins and cakes are simple enough, but it is difficult for her to refuse the entreaties of the poor man whose donkey has dropped part of his load or the women who need assistance with their weaving or the dying man who calls pitifully after her for succor. Shutting out the sad calls from those in need, Psyche pushes onward and downward. This journey no one can make for her. She alone can make it, and in spite of temptations to abandon her errand, she succeeds. Thank goodness for the tower and its counsel!

A talking tower? Refusing to help those in need? A journey to the underworld? What is this all about? Well, most significant transitions—the sort of inner change that Psyche is dealing with—involve a time in hell. You go down before you come up. And most of these journeys must be taken alone. All our habits of caring for others (and seeing ourselves as people who would care for others) become self-defeating. We need to resist the old impulses to take care of others and instead to pay attention during this time to what we are doing and why we are doing it. We are going where we have to go if we are to do the god's bidding. Having left behind a life that we have outgrown, we must continue the transition process to find our new life.

And the tower? Why, after all the previous help from insects and birds and growing things, does this aid come from a human construct, an inanimate object? It seems that, in the end, one needs that kind of assistance—that one's own deeper and unconscious resources are essential, but that they stop short of the goal. When one is going down the dark path into hell, some conscious plans must be made. The result is paradoxical—as was my urging you to trust your own inner process, and then my advice on what to do. So be it. Both are essential. And in the dark times, one may have little but that dimly remembered advice to go on.

It would be nice to say that Amor was waiting when Psyche reappeared, but he was not. In fact, things took an apparently bad turn at that very point. Back in the land of the living, Psyche looked indecisively at the box of magic ointment in her hand. She was tempted to open the box. Anything so valuable must be wonderful. Why should Aphrodite get it all? So she opened it. But the power of the content was too much for a mortal, and Psyche was overcome and collapsed.

Everything in a myth points to a purpose, and just as the earlier impulse to peek at her secret lover led to the quest that carried her to a new level of awareness, so this peek opened up immense power. That is always how it is in the wilderness of the neutral zone: One en-

counters there forms of energy and insight that are life transforming, but also just barely supportable. That is one reason why the old rituals were so important, for, like the tower, they gave direction and reassurance. That is why the sort of understanding that this book provides is so important, for without it you can be caught in fearful places that make no sense. So Psyche is not just overly curious when she lifts the lid of her treasure from the underworld. She is taking the final step to becoming aware of herself and gaining power for the new status and phase of her life. As with all people after important life transitions, she is going to be different.

No sooner has she fallen to the ground than Amor appeared and picked up the limp form and carried her up to Olympus. There, after due deliberation, Psyche was made immortal. She and Amor were married, and they lived happily ever after. . . .

. . . Or until the next major life transition, whichever came first.

NOTES

PART I

1. Daniel J. Boorstin, *The Americans: The National Experience* (New York: Random House, 1965), 92–93. Part 2, titled "The Transients," is an interesting historical background to the present study.

2. Quoted in G. W. Pierson, *Tocqueville and Beaumont in America* (New York: Oxford University Press, 1938), 119.

3. *The Complete Poetical Works of Henry Wadsworth Longfellow* (Boston: Houghton Mifflin, 1893), 296.

4. Alvin Toffler, *Future Shock* (New York: Bantam Books, 1970), 12.

CHAPTER 1

1. Lewis Carroll, *Alice's Adventures in Wonderland* (New York: Signet Books, 1960), 47.

2. Mircea Eliade, *Rites and Symbols of Initiation,* trans. Willard Trask (New York: Harper & Row, 1965), 31.

3. This rating scale was first published in the *Journal of Psychosomatic Research* 11 (1967): 213–218. It has been reprinted in many places since, including newspapers and magazines; and as a pamphlet called *Stress,* published in 1974 by Blue Cross Association, Chicago.

CHAPTER 2

1. Erik H. Erikson, *Identity, Youth, and Crisis* (New York: W. W. Norton, 1968), 128–135.

2. Daniel J. Levinson, *The Seasons of a Man's Life* (New York: Knopf, 1978), 78–84.

3. Ibid., 84–89; and Roger Gould, *Transformations* (New York: Simon and Schuster, 1978), 153–215.

4. The most convenient summary of Buhler's work is in an article by one of her coworkers, Else Frnekel-Brunswik. Titled "Adjustment and Reorientation in the Course of the Life Span," it is printed in Bernice L. Neugraten, ed., *Middle Age and Aging* (Chicago: University of Chicago Press, 1968), 77–84.

5. Levinson, 141.

6. For information about late bloomers and people who maintained a high level of productivity into the later years, see John A. B. McLeish, *The Ulyssean Adult: Creativity in the Middle and Later Years* (Toronto: McGraw-Hill-Ryerson, 1976).

7. Huston Smith, *The Religions of Man* (New York: Mentor Books, 1958), 64.

8. C. G. Jung, *Psychological Reflections*, ed. Jolande Jacobi (New York: Harper & Row, 1953), 119.

9. C. G. Jung, *Modern Man in Search of a Soul* (New York: Harcourt Brace, 1933), 107. More systematic and modern research suggests something that—if not so metaphorical—is similar. For example, Bernice Neugarten's "Adult Personality: Toward a Psychology of the Life Cycle" (in Neugarten, *Middle Age*, 140) where she writes, "Important differences exist between men and women as they age. Men seem to become more receptive to affiliative and nurturant promptings; women more responsive toward and less guilty about aggressive and egocentric impulses."

10. McLeish, *The Ulyssean Adult*.

11. Quoted in A. L. Vischer, *On Growing Old*, trans. Gerald Onn (Boston: Houghton Mifflin, 1967), 169.

CHAPTER 3

1. See Rosalie Maggio, *Quotations By Women* (Boston: Beacon Press, 1992), 203.

2. Ibid., 43.

CHAPTER 4

1. "Career transition" has come to be synonymous with career *change* or simply the loss of a job. That is unfortunate, for it makes it difficult to talk about *transitions within careers*—whether those occur because of an externally driven change or because of an inner shift as we move from one chapter of our lives to the next. Once again, it is important to keep the difference between *change* and *transition* clear. The *change* is a shift in one's situation: a relocation, a promotion, a new position, a new boss, a new retirement plan, or a new technology. The *transition* is the psychological process of disengagement from the old, going through the nowhere between old and new, and then embracing and identifying with the new. The *transition* may be the result of a *change*—either at work or at home—but it may also be simply one of those inner periods of reorientation and renewal (like the "mid-life transition")

that is built right into the lifetime. In the previous chapter, we talked about transitions within the context of a relationship, and in this chapter we are discussing transitions that take place in careers. The term *career transition* does not refer to career change or job loss.

2. For more on the distinctive contribution of people in the final chapter of their lives, see the chapter titled "Transition and Elderhood," in William Bridges, *The Way of Transition* (Cambridge, Mass.: Perseus Publishing, 2000), 179–199.

3. Ibid., 197.

4. If your transition involves the need to find new work and a new source of income, you would find another of my books helpful. That is *Creating You & Co.* (Cambridge, Mass.: Perseus Publishing, 1997).

PART II

1. Mircea Eliade, *The Sacred and the Profance*, trans. Willard Trask (New York: Harcourt, Brace, Jovanovich, 1959), 208–209.

2. For component details see Arnold van Gennep, *Rites of Passage*, trans. Monika B. Vizedom and Gabrielle L. Chaffee (Chicago: University of Chicago Press, 1960); Mircea Eliade, *Rites and Symbols of Initiation*, trans. Willard Trask (New York: Harper & Row, 1965); Victor W. Turner, *The Ritual Process* (Chicago: Aldine, 1969); and Peter Radin, *Primitive Religion* (Magnolia, Mass.: Peter Smith, 1957).

3. Van Gennep, *Rites*, 10–11.

CHAPTER 5

1. T. S. Eliot, *Four Quartets* (New York: Harcourt, Brace 1943), 38.

2. From a Zen story adapted by Paul Reps; in *Zen Flesh, Zen Bones* (New York: Anchor Books, n.d.), 18.

3. The examples come from Sam D. Gill, "Disenchantment," *Parabola* (Summer 1976): 6–13.

4. Elisabeth Kubler-Ross, *On Death and Dying* (New York: Macmillan, 1969), 38–137.

5. Mircea Eliade, *Myths, Dreams and Mysteries*, trans. Philip Mairet (New York, Harper & Row, 1967), 224.

CHAPTER 6

1. Lao Tzu, *Tao Te Ching*, trans. D. C. Lau (Middlesex, England: Penguin Books, 1963).

2. Carlos Castaneda, *The Teachings of Don Juan* (New York: Ballantine Books, 1968), 110.

3. This quotation and an extended account of Tolstoy's crisis appear in his autobiographical work, *A Confession*, trans. Aylmer Maude (London: Oxford University Press, 1940).

4. Mircea Eliade, *Myths, Dreams, and Mysteries*, trans. Philip Mairet (New York: Harper and Row, 1967), 80.

5. Arnold van Gennep, *Rites of Passage*, trans. Monika B. Vizedom and Gabrielle L. Chaffee (Chicago: University of Chicago Press), 182.

6. "Nature," The Complete Works of Ralph Waldo Emerson, vol. 1 (Boston: Houghton Mifflin, 1903), 4.

7. George Orwell, *1984* (New York: Signet Books, 1949), 189.

8. This material on *wanting* was drawn from the seminars of James Bugental.

9. A book that explores this need and how it is reflected in the Judeo-Christian idea of the *sabbath* is Wayne Muller, *Sabbath: Restoring the Ancient Rhythm of Rest and Delight* (New York: Bantam), 1999.

10. Lewis Carroll, *Alice's Adventures in Wonderland* (New York: Signet Books, 1960), 27.

11. Arnold Toynbee, *A Study of History*, abridged by D.C. Somervell (New York: Oxford University Press, 1947), 217–230.

CHAPTER 7

1. Horace, "To Lollius," *Epistles*, Book I:2.

2. John Galsworthy, *Over the River* (London: William Heineman, 1933), 4.

3. Mircea Eliade, *Myths, Dreams and Mysteries*, trans. Philip Mairet (New York: Harper & Row, 1967), 48.

4. Joseph P. Lash, *Eleanor and Franklin* (New York: W. W. Norton, 1971), 238.

EPILOGUE

1. Ralph Waldo Emerson, *The Journals and Miscellaneous Notebooks of Ralph Waldo Emerson*, vol. 5, ed. Merton M. Sealts, Jr. (Cambridge, Mass.: Harvard University Press, 1965), 38.

2. This tale, originally told by the Latin writer Apulieus, has been studied, though not from this perspective, by several modern psychologists who used it to illustrate aspects of feminine psychology. See Robert A. Johnson, *She: Understanding Feminine Psychology* (New York: Harper & Row, 1976), and Erich Neumann, *Amor and Psyche* (Princeton: Princeton University Press, 1956).

INDEX